JULIA Roberts

Colin MacLean

ICON
PRESS

First printed in 2005 10 9 8 7 6 5 4 3 2 1

Printed in Canada

The Publisher: Icon Press, an imprint of Folklore Publishing

Website: www.folklorepublishing.com

Library and Archives Canada Cataloguing in Publication

MacLean, Colin, 1936–
Julia Roberts: more than a pretty woman / Colin MacLean

(Star biographies)
Includes bibliographical references.
ISBN 1-894864-23-9

1. Roberts, Julia, 1967–. 2. Motion picture actors and actresses—United States—Biography. I. Title. II. Series.

PN2287.R63M32 2005 791.4302'8'092 C2005-900605-6

Project Director: Faye Boer
Project Editor: Rachelle Delaney & Nicholle Carrière
Production: Linda Bolger, Trina Koscielnuk
Cover Design: Valentino
Book Design: Anne & Dion
Cover Image: Courtesy of International Communications Systems

Photography credits: Every effort has been made to accurately credit the sources of photographs. Any errors or omissions should be directed to the publisher for changes in future editions. Photographs courtesy of International Communications Systems.

We acknowledge the support of the Alberta Foundation for the Arts for our publishing program.

PC:P6

Alberta Foundation for the Arts

Table of Contents

Dedication

To Stefanie, Roxanne, Larissa, Jennifer and Halia, who shared a conviction that it was never only a movie.

Introduction

Intimations

The first time I talked with Julia Roberts, she was in tears.

I walked into the posh Four Seasons Hotel room in Los Angeles to find the budding superstar wiping her eyes with a tissue. She assured me that she was okay, just overcome by what had just happened.

I had been waiting outside her door to be ushered in when a great hulk of a man appeared and asked if he could just nip in to ask Ms. Roberts a quick question. Since the fellow was quite unmistakably Gene Hackman, I was not about to say no. He disappeared into the room and, true to his word, reappeared moments later, mumbled thank you and held the door open for me.

"I can't believe what just happened," said the obviously overcome Roberts. "I can't believe that Gene Hackman waited outside my door to ask me to lunch."

I had arrived to discuss the film *Sleeping with the Enemy*, a tale of spousal abuse and Roberts' first film to be released after her monumental 1990 hit *Pretty Woman.* She didn't yet perceive herself as a superstar and hence was emotionally overwhelmed by the invitation from Hackman.

Or so I thought.

Like many events in the chaotic life of this confounding and complex woman, that moment was not as simple as it seemed. Roberts had arrived at the interview that morning wound as tight as a violin string. Although she was being paid $1 million for her solo starring role, she was still unproven at the box office—critics mused that Pretty Woman could have been just a flash in the pan. The shoot for *Sleeping with the Enemy* had been long and grueling. Julia had been injured twice while filming the physically demanding scenes, when carefully planned blows had gone wrong. She remembered: "It's not easy playing someone who is tormented and abused. I got

Sleeping with the Enemy (1991)

thrown around a lot, mentally and physically, and during rehearsals I would often have to walk out to get some air. It was just too intense." The young actress had yet to learn to hang her emotions on the dressing room door when she left the shoot at night. And, unknown to most everyone, Roberts had her lover-du-jour, Kiefer Sutherland, stashed away in a nearby hotel room. Although she kept proclaiming her undying love for the Canadian-born actor, the relationship was beginning to show cracks that would lead to one of the most celebrated breakups in movie history.

Julia Roberts was at the center of another of the emotional and physical firestorms that had marked her life since childhood.

No wonder she was in tears.

So much has been written about Julia Roberts that it's almost impossible to determine where the media-manufactured image of the superstar leaves off and reality begins. She lives so much in a goldfish bowl that it is difficult to disassociate her private life from her public existence. She is, possibly, the most widely publicized young woman of modern times. There is no doubting the love affair that exists between this gifted but deeply insecure star and her audiences, who can't seem to get enough of her.

Although she has made many films, Roberts will always be associated with her first big hit *Pretty Woman.* Her role as the sanitized prostitute Viv Ward, who is picked up by businessman Richard Gere to be his platonic companion for a week of social events, was the sort of star-making turn that actresses search a lifetime to find. Roberts was lucky enough to be offered it when she was only 22 years old. But one good role does not a star make, as shown by the many able actresses who have come and gone while Robert's celestial orb continues to sparkle. Simply put, the movie industry has not been able to mint another female star that twinkles with her intensity. Not only has she spent years at the top of the salary scale, but she is the only actress capable of commanding a fee commensurate to (and often surpassing) the wages of her male co-stars.

Like many teenagers before her, Roberts felt awkward and unattractive in her high school years. Perhaps that is why, even now, she seems unimpressed with her own image, although she is widely

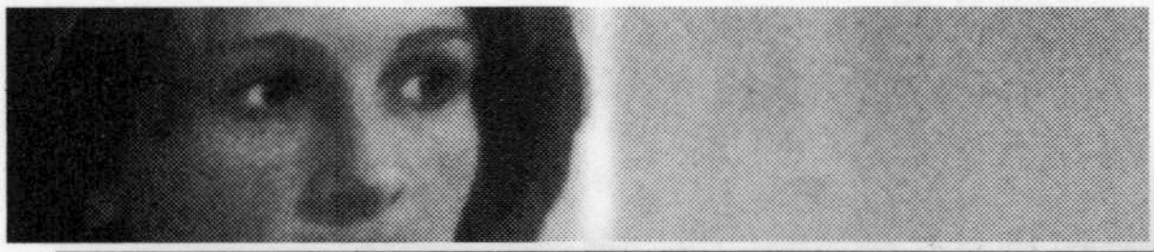

JULIA FAN FACT

Julia is 5 feet 9 inches tall and weighs 121 pounds. Her eyes are brown (on certain days hazel). "My real hair color is a kind of dark blonde," she once said. "Now I just have mood hair."

regarded as one of the most beautiful women in the world. She often projects an impression of life-affirming joy, but as anyone who has seen her in her best roles will attest, there is an ineffable feeling of vulnerability that lurks about those huge hazel eyes. Male audiences respond to her earthy sexiness and accessibility; women have an instinctive sense that she'd make a great buddy. Like Audrey Hepburn, Julia Roberts has an atypical beauty. Pencil thin and long legged with a thick, curly, auburn mane, she looks more coltish than elegant. She sparkles onscreen with a special mischievous charm, augmented by the broad grin and braying laugh that the camera loves.

Julia's disordered personal life has fueled several biographies, countless magazine stories and many conversations around the water cooler. We can't seem to get enough of her. Her dysfunctional childhood is the stuff of endless speculation and could serve as the basis for volumes of learned psychological studies.

Three kinds of actresses exist in Hollywood. The first includes the great thespians that search their souls for authentic emotions. The second category is made up of comely young ladies who rely largely on their beauty to drive their careers. Then there is the third category, and these are rare creatures indeed. They have an intangible quality that is impossible to define. Their larger-than-life personalities are often greater than the vehicles in which they appear. They possess both beauty and talent. They are the stars. Like Ingrid Bergman, Bette Davis and Marilyn Monroe, Julia Roberts is a star.

★★★

chapter 1

surviving your Family

Nineteen sixty-seven—a year of turmoil in the United States. It began with American troops engaged in hand-to-hand battle with the Viet Cong in the Mekong Delta of Vietnam. Protests were springing up all over the U.S. Frank Sinatra won the Grammy for *Strangers in the Night.* At the movies you'd find *The Graduate, Bonnie and Clyde, Guess Who's Coming to Dinner* and the Oscar-winning *In the Heat of the Night.* On television, we were watching *The Lawrence Welk Show, Mannix, My Three Sons* and *Hogan's Heroes.*

On October 21, tens of thousands of Americans marched in Washington to protest the Vietnam War. And four days later, Julia Fiona Roberts, the third child of Walter and Betty Roberts, was born in Crawford Long Hospital in downtown Atlanta, Georgia.

Julia's mother, Betty Lou, was a short, pretty blonde. Betty wanted to study drama, but her profligate father spent money as fast as he earned it. So she turned to an institution that would give her an education for nothing—the armed forces. In August 1953, she enlisted in the American Air Force and was stationed at Keesler Air Force Base in Biloxi, Mississippi. There she pursued her interests in performing by appearing in local productions.

And there she met Airman First Class Walter Grady Roberts.

Walter Grady Roberts was born on Christmas Day 1933, in Atlanta. His father Tom was a pragmatic type who worked in construction and enjoyed a steady progression to a supervisory position throughout his 46-year career with the same company. Young Walter, however, was as artistic and creative as his father was hard working and matter-of-fact. When his father decided that Walter was "too intellectual" and declined to send him to college, Walter, too, joined the Air Force and found himself posted to Biloxi.

Betty and Walter met in a production of George S. Kaufman and Moss Hart's *George Washington Slept Here.* Soon, the relationship between Walter and Betty spilled off the stage and into their private lives.

To attempt to understand Julia Roberts, their complex, difficult and emotionally unstable third child, you must look at the gothic familial influences that shaped her childhood. It's not a pretty picture but it's certainly instructive.

Only a few months after their romantic meeting behind the footlights, Walter and Betty decided to get married, and one year later, they celebrated the birth of their first child, Eric. After their service stints ended, the growing family moved to New Orleans, where Walter attended Tulane University and studied English literature and psychology. Walter, with his experience and training, felt superior to everyone around him, including his professors. He could barely keep his fiery temper in control, and finally stalked out of the university, believing his professors had nothing to teach him.

In May 1965, Walter and Betty had their second child, Lisa Billingsley Roberts. That same year, Walter came up with an idea—he would conduct local actors' and writers' workshops on the ground floor of their home.

So when baby Julia arrived two years later, the place was humming with actors and others interested in theater. One of the participants was Julia's now 11-year-old brother Eric.

So when baby Julia arrived two years later, the place was humming with actors and others interested in theater.

Eric had a pronounced stutter and was unable to express himself effectively—except on stage. He told an interviewer in later years: "My dad always found ways of making acting magical to me. He would wake me up in the middle of the night to show me something special on television. And, I learned in grade school, if I memorized something, I wouldn't stutter, which made acting a cure." Eric began to memorize large parts of his homework in case he was called on to read in class: "If I didn't get it memorized first, I thought I would stutter, and everyone would laugh." Eric's plan usually worked well, except when the teacher changed the lesson plan and called on the terrified scholar to read something he had not committed to memory. "I used to get in fights over it," he recalled. "I'd fight until I was dead." Eric grew to idolize his father, a relationship that would eventually contribute to a split with his youngest sister.

Meanwhile, Walter's Actor's Studio was showing great promise. Although she was only two years old, Julia maintained in later years: "I still have traces of memory from when I was little—of watching this magical world unfold in front of me." Walter was difficult and demanding, but most of his performers adored him. Perhaps it was because they were young, relatively unsophisticated and nonthreatening to their mentor.

But the shining path that Walter and Betty set out on slowly crumbled into a rocky road. The pressures of running the workshop and earning enough money to keep the family going, together with rumors of Betty's infidelity, proved too much for their relationship to withstand. On June 13, 1971, Betty filed for divorce. The break seemed civil, even amicable, with little evidence of the bitterness to come.

Although she was only two years old, Julia maintained in later years: "I still have traces of memory from when I was little—of watching this magical world unfold in front of me."

Betty Lou Roberts couldn't have felt too broken up over the split. Only a month after the divorce was finalized, she had taken up with a man named Michael Motes. Although Eric has never spoken about it in public, members of the Roberts extended family maintain that Eric came home early one day after school and found Betty in bed with Motes when she was still married to Eric's father. At any rate, Betty and Michael Motes moved in together, and the courts decided that Eric, Lisa and Julia should live with their mother. Motes seemed like a strange partner for the fun-loving Betty. Next to Walter's bohemian good looks, Motes was a large fellow with a pale complexion and horn-rimmed glasses. He had lost much of his hair and compensated by wearing cheap wigs.

Betty married Michael Motes in September 1972.

But things started to go terribly wrong. The seemingly amicable split turned acrimonious. In 1998, Eric told an interviewer: "Obviously my mother wanted to have a relationship and wanted to take care of her children, but I don't think she knew what she was getting into when she agreed to marry Motes. It was common knowledge where we lived that Motes was a freak. He would have stood out in a crowd of ten thousand. I don't know whether he married my mother to get close to the children or not, but clearly, marrying him was not a good or a healthy thing for her or her children. Our mother's husband terrorized and abused me, and I feel he terrorized my sisters Lisa and Julia as well."

Eric's allegations are supported by the fact that Julia will not speak of Motes in interviews, no matter how probing the journalist. She has only offered: "After my parents divorced, my mother my sister and I moved to Smyrna (Georgia)." (Note that she doesn't refer to her brother either.) Walter soon filed to regain possession of his children. He alleged that Motes had

> **In 1998, Eric told an interviewer: "...Our mother's husband terrorized and abused me, and I feel he terrorized my sisters Lisa and Julia as well."**

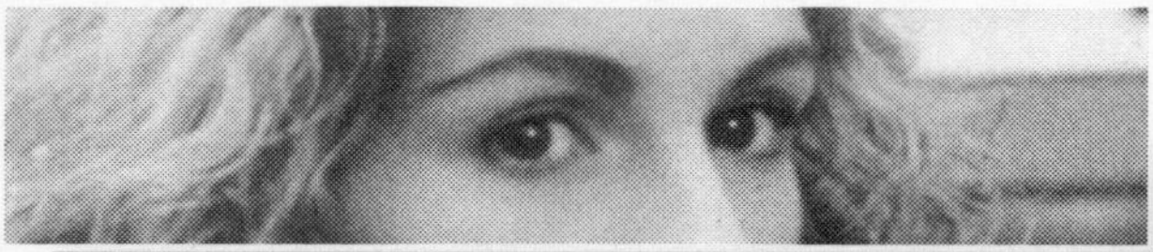

JULIA FAN FACT

Early in her career, Julia commented to *Rolling Stone*: "I come from a real touchy family. A lotta hugging, a lotta kissing, a lotta love."
"Julia is in denial," Eric observed tersely when he read her statement. Years later, in an unguarded moment, Julia admitted: "We all had to grow up fast."

struck and injured Eric "with no cause," ordered Eric out of the house and refused him care. On the night he was thrown out, the 16-year-old Eric walked, in a pouring rainstorm, from Smyrna to Atlanta—a distance of about 10 miles. He was looking for his father, but the elder Roberts was not home, and the teen ended up at his father's girlfriend's mother's home for the night.

Betty filed a countersuit that charged Walter with stealing furniture and other objects from the house they had shared—objects that had been ceded to Betty. The court split up the family. Lisa and Julia remained with Betty and Michael, and Eric went to live with his father.

Later, Eric observed wearily: "I grew up in a dysfunctional home. Everybody hated each other and made it clear."

The Motes divorced nine years after their marriage.

In 1974, Walter tried again to gain more access to his daughters, but the court granted him just one 15-minute conversation with the girls on Wednesday nights. Betty intercepted all the letters and presents he sent, destroyed them and told the kids that their father had forgotten them.

During this time, Julia formed a close relationship with her sister Lisa. The two huddled together for emotional support during these difficult times and turned to each other when their family seemed to be careening out of control.

The temptation to apply a bit of pop psychology to this emotional morass is strong. As an adult, Julia Roberts dreads confrontation. Said one observer: "Julia avoids conflict at all costs, even with those she's close to. The moment you hear her arguing with someone—even a lover—you can start ticking the moments until it's over."

Eric, who has led an extremely troubled life and sometimes seems to be seeking therapy in public pronouncements, told an interviewer in 1998: "Children who grow up in a troubled environment usually blame themselves for their pain. You figure you have done something bad to have suffered so. You come to think you have deserved the pain. That guilt leads to self-destructive behavior."

Journalist Leon Wegner penned a profile of Eric in a 1998 issue of the British magazine *Here!* He wrote: "When Julia was 10, living with her mom and stepfather in Smyrna, Georgia, Motes began sexually molesting a teenage boy, often in the family home. Eric claims Mote's behavior was not only directed towards strangers' children. He was terrified of his stepfather and believes that living in Mote's household during their formative years has had a profound effect on Julia and himself."

Eric soon moved away and found that his intensity, stark good looks and acting skills all opened doors. Julia followed not far behind, but the siblings' careers, like their lives, diverged onto very different paths.

★★★

chapter 2

The Ugly Duckling

In September 1980, Julia Roberts enrolled in the Griffin Middle School in Smyrna, Georgia. She wanted to be a veterinarian. Her mom remembered: "That's all Julia talked about for a long time. She still adores animals—especially dogs."

Julia said of that early passion: "I thought I was Dr. Doolittle. I was convinced I could talk to animals. But then I went to school and discovered science, which I hated, and that went out the window." But her love for animals never stopped—she adopted a stray dog on the set of *Pretty Woman* and surrounds herself with dogs and horses at her Taos, New Mexico, ranch today.

"I thought I was Dr. Doolittle. I was convinced I could talk to animals. But then I went to school and discovered science, which I hated, and that went out the window."

By the time she entered Campbell High School three years later, her dreams had changed, and she was determined to be a journalist. The young high school junior showed few signs of the breathtaking beauty she would become. In fact, Julia considered herself an ugly duckling. She wore thick eyeglasses and had braces to correct a gap in her front teeth ("You could stick a Popsicle stick between them") and buck teeth that resulted from sucking her thumb as a child. The generous mouth and "bee-stung" lips, which would later influence generations of young women, were a source of embarrassment for Julia—her fellow students teased her relentlessly about them. She was taller than most of the boys and felt uncoordinated and ungainly. She was an average scholar.

In 1991, the grubby *National Enquirer* tabloid ran an article that described Julia as being boy crazy in high school. It stated that her nickname was "Hot Pants Roberts." Not so, says a student who shared his high school

Satisfaction (1988)

years with Julia. "There were some girls in high school who were aggressive. She was wholesome and beautiful and sexy in her own right, but she was not a floozy. She was not a prissy girl. She was a southern-belle type—very preppy."

In short, Julia was a fairly normal high school student with little to make her stand out or indicate that she would ever excel. "In high school," she said, "I was like everybody else. I had my girlfriends. I did sports. I wasn't really great at anything—just middle of the road. A basic kid. I enjoyed school, but somehow I never really fit in." She was a busy student, treasurer for the school council and a member of the girl's tennis team. The school had no drama club.

Julia wasn't one to sit at home reading romance novels, though. She had a number of the usual high school relationships that culminated with losing her virginity to one Keith Leeper. Leeper was two years her senior and was standing at the bar in a disco when Julia came over and remarked that he looked like Sting.

"I asked her to dance, and we exchanged numbers. She was a good kisser," he later disclosed. As reported in various biographies and magazine stories, the event itself took place when Julia was 16 at a Christmas party in the Leeper home on December 12, 1983. "We were alone and kissing," is the way Leeper remembers it. "It wasn't anything planned. The timing was right. I took her by the hand and led her upstairs to my bedroom. We stayed there for about an hour before rejoining the party. She didn't tell me until later that it was the first time."

During the next few months the two would drive off in his pickup truck and park on a remote road where they would make love." I saw her differently after we had sex," Leeper says. "I started to fall in love with her, but then we also became best friends. It was puppy love at first."

But one aspect of her life made her unique—her brother was a movie star.

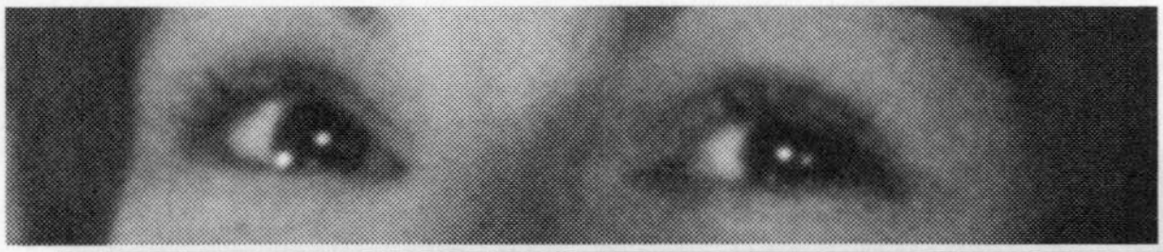

JULIA FAN FACT

With her family's economic circumstances, Julia had to work while attending high school. She sold pizza and ice cream, and worked in a movie theater and at the Piggly Wiggly supermarket.

But one aspect of her life made her unique—her brother was a movie star. While the rest of her classmates traveled south to the beaches of Florida for holidays, Julia went north to see her brother, the actor, in New York. In her senior year, Eric flew her to Australia to be with him on the set of *The Coca-Cola Kid.* The wonderful trip was capped by an encounter with Billy Idol on the flight. And when she got home, Julia found that Eric had bought her a present—a Volkswagen Beetle.

In 1973, Eric Roberts set out on the career path his father had pushed him towards since he was a child. Walter Roberts was determined that his son would succeed. Walter moved into a small apartment and saved every cent he could to send Eric to the prestigious Royal Academy of Dramatic Arts in England. After two years in London, Eric moved to New York to pursue his studies. Even then, he was a troubled young man given to bouts of depression, which he fought with an increasing dependency on liquor and drugs. But he hung on, landed a few off-Broadway roles and became a regular on the soap opera *Another World,* until he disagreed violently with his producers and was fired. Eric was muscular, intense, handsome and talented, and his career was burgeoning. He auditioned for a major role in the feature film *King of the Gypsies* and nailed it. The producing company, Paramount Pictures, saw him as "a star of the future" and spent millions promoting him as the new rebel actor—the next Montgomery Clift or James Dean.

Walter Roberts died on December 7, 1977, of throat cancer. Eric was there, of course. Betty did not attend the funeral, but she did allow Julia and Lisa to go.

Julia began to harbor dreams of being a Broadway actress. After all, her brother had shown that it could be done. She said: "I had a restlessness without focus, an urgency, an anxiety, like something's going to break." Early in 1985, Julia packed her life into the Volkswagen and pointed it north, up the New Jersey Turnpike, towards New York City. It took her 14 hours of nonstop driving before she arrived at her brother's lavish apartment in Greenwich Village. After a few days, she moved in with her sister Lisa who, two years before, had also left for the city, looking for her big break in theater. The two shared a small apartment near Greenwich Village. "Lisa really cushioned a lot of things for me," said Julia, looking back many years later. "I always considered her fearless. When we were kids, I always thought she'd protect me if I was scared. And in New York at 17, it was the same thing."

Julia spread her wings upon arriving in New York. She abandoned her attempts at being a well-dressed, if off-the-rack teen queen and adopted a bag lady, proto-grunge look. She carried this fashion statement with her for many years, even after she became one of the highest-paid actors in Hollywood. It wasn't long before she had generated a reputation of being a "party girl." A friend was quoted to say: "She had a lot of friends—mostly boyfriends. She had a lot of flings—at least four I know of in New York." Another friend chimed in: "She was wild, free spirited—always up for a good time."

Julia also used her brother's contacts to meet the right people. One was agent Mary Sames, who remembered their first meeting, where a scruffy Julia showed up in her office. "She seemed to be so innocent, so completely without guile and yet at the same time so guarded, so wary, that I was fascinated by what I perceived to be a unique personality. I mean, here was this free spirit, this breathtakingly beautiful young girl who was nevertheless shy and awkward and gave off the vibes of a fragile bird." Sames also perceived that Julia would be a high-maintenance client. "I realized instantly that this demure, shy, waif-like girl sitting across from me needed someone special and kindhearted to take care of her—that she was

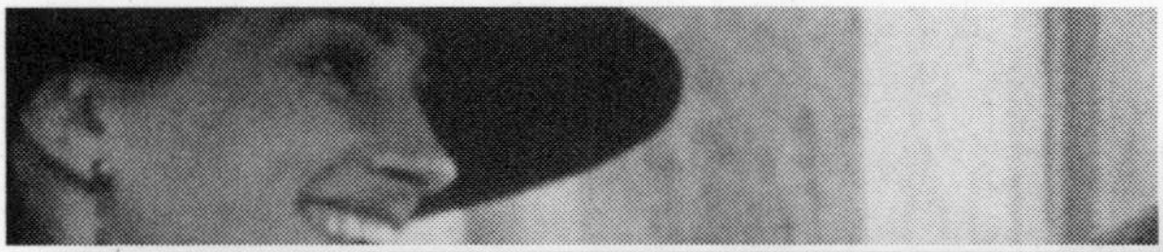

JULIA FAN FACT

Julia Roberts was known in these years as Jules or Julie. When she appeared in her first film shot under the Screen Actor's Guild, she was told she had to register a name. A Julie Roberts already existed on the roster, so with the advice of her mother, she registered as Julia Roberts. The irony is that Julia Roberts is her birth name—she is one of the few actors who adopted her real name for the movies.

going to need 24-hours-a-day nurturing. And frankly, I didn't have it in me at the time." So she handed the kid off to Bob McGowan, who was beginning a career as a personal manager. McGowan then became Julia's keeper. He loaned her money and paid her rent (although he never knew where she lived). He persuaded his young charge to take acting lessons and speech therapy because she spoke with a southern accent as thick as a Georgia swamp. It didn't take. Julia later remarked: "I went to acting class a few times, but it never seemed conducive to what I wanted to do...Things just sort of happened. Basically, I've learned on the job. I don't know quite what I'm doing until it's done."

Meanwhile, Eric's career was already in free fall. After a promising start, he proved too difficult for many producers to deal with. He turned down major roles because he didn't think they were right for him. When he refused the lead in *An Officer and a Gentleman,* Richard Gere accepted the role and became a major star. In 1983, Eric shone as the doomed Paul Snider, the seedy husband/manager of Playboy bunny Dorothy Stratton, in Bob Fosse's *Star 80.* He followed up that role with an Oscar nomination for his standout work in *Runaway Train,* but his constant battle with depression, drugs and alcohol was beginning to take a toll. In 1981, he was involved in a near-fatal car accident that ravaged his face and, for a while, left him unable to remember lines. Shortly before the accident, he had suggested to the producers of a small film in which he was starring that Julia be given the role of his sister—or so the story goes. Many participants, from agents to producers, have taken the credit for the idea. Even Julia, who was becoming increasingly alienated from her brother, claimed she won the role in an audition, not even knowing he was the star.

During this time, the chasm that would tear the family apart became apparent. Julia had seldom witnessed her brother's erratic and self-destructive behavior back home in Smyrna, but living in the same city and working in the same industry allowed her to see it close up. Some reports maintain that Julia once went to Eric's apartment and found him in a stupor. In tears, she begged him to let her help. Now that she was making some money herself, she offered to fly him to the Betty Ford Clinic where he could dry out. Eric refused.

"I tried to help him, but I couldn't get through," Julia said to a friend—one of the few times she spoke of her relationship with her brother. "I want to help, but I can't let him destroy me, too." Julia now gives Eric no credit for his help and never mentions him in interviews. He has not been invited to any of his sister's weddings. They have not spoken to each other—except through the media—in over a decade.

Meanwhile, Julia's star was rising. She was beginning to be noticed and was featured in several television programs.

Julia appeared as a bass guitar player in Aaron Spelling's film *Satisfaction.* To prepare for the role, she learned to play the instrument acceptably well. Her role as Daryle also called on her ability to play sexy. One character in the movie remarks: "On a good day Daryle is a slut."

It was on the set of *Satisfaction* that Julia began the first of a prodigious number of sexual relationships with her co-stars. Liam Neeson was an Irish character actor just beginning to make his way. In *Satisfaction,* he played an aging rock star turned bar

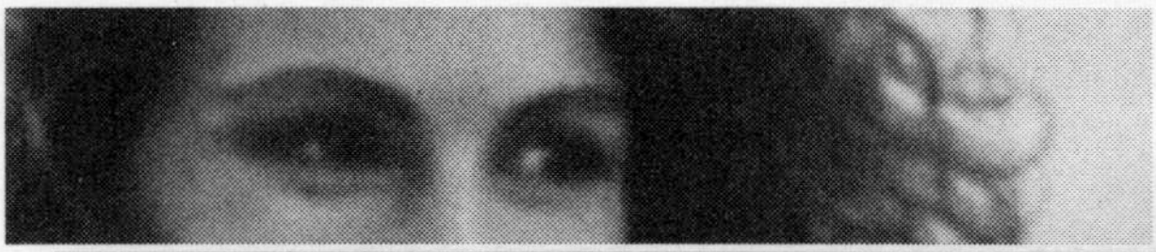

JULIA LOVE-LIFE UPDATE

For those who want to know about such things, many tabloid publications and learned biographies state that Neeson had a reputation (backed up by a number of high-profile girlfriends) of having been blessed with some very impressive plumbing and the ability to employ it with great skill.

owner who went back on the road one more time. Neeson, who would later triumph in *Schindler's List*, hated the film and refused to talk about it, grinding out "unsatisfactory. I don't intend to see it," when asked about his work in the movie. But the 35-year-old actor did like the 19-year-old girl on the bass guitar. A lot. In Ingrid Miller's biography of the actor, she quotes one of his friends as saying: "They were absolutely nuts about each other. They couldn't keep their hands off each other. It was incredible to watch. Liam is cool, but he was incredibly responsive to Julia. In contrast, she's a very tactile person. She seemed to spark off him, and she would be crawling all over him."

Julia and her co-star certainly didn't invent the offscreen romance—that movie tradition goes back to a time when the star system first began to develop in Hollywood. Making a movie is a little like being at war. The participants live in their own, often overwhelming, worlds and regard everyone outside as civilians. The pressures are real and, because of the nature of the art, emotions run high. Stars are often called upon to create intimate situations, and the passions generated for the camera are sometimes hard to turn off.

The fling flamed white hot for about a year before it began to fade. But Julia, fledgling movie star, was beginning to fly.

★★★

chapter 3

spreading her Wings

S*atisfaction* (later called *Girls of Summer* in an effort to disguise it) flopped. One Internet critic said: "What an awful, awful movie! Horrible. Horrendous. Although...Julia Roberts was really hot with her big '80s hair."

"It taught me a lot about what I hope never to do again in a movie," recalled Julia ruefully.

At that point in her accelerating career, each film Julia made was a major leap over the previous one. In 1988, she appeared as a featured player in an excellent HBO original film called *Baja Oklahoma*. She played Candy Hutchens, the 18-year-old daughter of Lesley Anne Warren's character, Juanita, who pines to be a country-and-western songwriter.

Julia began to establish the perimeters that would govern her life in the movies. She loved to hang out with the crew and lacked the barracuda attitude that often affects actors. She wasn't obsessed with acting. She was an interesting mix of being very real and natural and very focused. She knew what she wanted and where she was headed in terms of her career, and she felt confident that it would all happen at her pace.

Baja Oklahoma was so well received that it was released briefly to theaters before its run on television. Critic Leonard Maltin called it "lively" and "above average."

Three weeks after *Baja Oklahoma* wrapped, Julia flew to an audition in New York. The film would call on the expertise she had developed selling fast food at the mall in Smyrna. It was called *Mystic Pizza* and was a coming-of-age tale of three young women who work in a pizza parlor in Mystic, Connecticut.

When she arrived at the audition, Julia learned that she was to read for the part of Daisy Arugo, who was Portuguese. There were hundreds of young actresses vying for the part. Julia set about turning herself into a young woman of Portuguese descent and came up with an inspired twist, born of necessity and lack of money. She borrowed a suit from her manager Bob McGowan, which, in an effort to underline the earthy sexuality of the character, she wore at the reading without a bra or a blouse underneath. She also colored her hair with a mixture of mousse, hair dye and shoe polish. She wore her Walkman with Jimi Hendrix's live version of "Wild Thing" pumped up as loud as she could stand and played it over and over again in a desperate effort to draw on Hendrix's energy. Using every trick in her bottomless bag, she began to sing loudly to the tape, increasing the tension in the room. It escalated even more when she began to throw pens into the soundproofing tiles in the ceiling. "All the girls started getting very nervous, as if I had some kind of inner track or something," she chuckled.

Mystic Pizza (1988)

The reading itself, in front of director Daniel Petrie and producer Mark Levinson, went well until the actor she was playing opposite impulsively reached out to run his fingers through her hair and pulled his hand back to find it stained black. Everyone in the room broke up. "Julia was real smart to put that rinse in her hair and make it jet black, like the color of the Portuguese character she played in the film," laughed Petrie when asked about it later. "She was exactly what I needed for the role—unpredictable and willing to take chances, fiery, spirited and yet very real." Soon thereafter, Julia found herself in Mystic along with co-stars Annabeth Gish and Lili Taylor. Her salary was set at $50,000.

Once again, Julia established a strong relationship with the crew, which, even if it changed from shoot to shoot, grew to be a kind of protective family for her. She had to put a bit of weight on her lean frame for the role, which delighted her co-workers behind the camera.

Mystic Pizza, by all accounts, was a happy shoot. Everyone believed in the project and got along famously. Julia celebrated her 20th birthday on October 28, 1987. She didn't want to call attention to herself, so she didn't tell anyone, but somehow, someone found out and, in midafternoon, her buddies on the crew wheeled out a huge cake shaped like a pizza and topped with 20 candles. Julia was overwhelmed, blushed crimson, dissolved

"She was exactly what I needed for the role—unpredictable and willing to take chances, fiery, spirited and yet very real."

into tears and ran from the set. She returned in a few minutes. "I'm shy, and I'm an extrovert," she explained trying to rationalize the two conflicting elements of her personality. "So everyone seems to get a kick out of the fact that I blush easily. But I do. Certain things make me go, 'Well, I've got to run. See you later…'"

On the set, Julia developed a habit that she would abandon in later shoots. She fretted the part. She kept going over and over her lines trying to wring every nuance out of them. That approach made her readings too studied. Petrie noted the change. "She had a wonderful spontaneity onscreen that really makes her light up," he commented. "Most actors have it in their eyes. But Julia has it in her eyes, her face, everywhere. She's the kind of actor you want to shoot without a rehearsal because she's so quirky you never know what you're going to get."

Petrie may have been the first director to publicly observe that trait in Julia, but he would certainly not be the last. Julia herself, in a moment of self-awareness, once told a national audience on the television program *Inside the Actor's Studio*: " I have only so many chances of having it come out exactly the way I want it, and I don't want those to happen in the seven takes that we rehearse it and the cameras not rolling. I'm afraid there are only so many in there, so better go get 'em."

Mystic Pizza was released on the October 21, 1988. The reviews were mixed, but the film grossed $14 million at the box office on an original budget of $3.5 million. Not bad for a small, unheralded movie with no marquee stars. Roger Ebert commented on the movie's "effortless charm" and went on to say: "Roberts is a major beauty with a fierce energy."

After the release of the film and Julia's subsequent growing fame, she received a small taste of the media frenzy to come. Back home in Smyrna, she and her mother decided to take in a movie. Julia was ensconced in the ladies' room when she

"She's the kind of actor you want to shoot without a rehearsal because she's so quirky you never know what you're going to get."

heard a woman's voice loudly calling, "Excuse me, girl in stall number one. Weren't you in *Mystic Pizza*?"

"Yeah," said the reluctant star.

"Can I have your autograph, please?" said the voice. A pen and a piece of paper appeared under the stall door.

"I don't think now is the right time," Julia bristled.

Back in New York, Julia's relationship with Neeson was growing volatile. The two smokers puffed like smokestacks, swore like sailors on shore leave and pursued their frequent arguments at high volumes. And while the cracks were beginning to show in their relationship, across town, brother Eric was completely flaming out—again.

Early on the morning of December 3, 1987, a woman flagged down a patrol car near an apartment building on West 81st in New York. When the two cops entered the building they found the source of the disruption—Eric Roberts, very drunk and pounding on the door of a woman who lived there. Terrified, the unidentified woman called a friend, who had run out and stopped the cop car. Eric attacked the officers, almost decking one with a wild blow. When he was finally subdued and booked, the police found marijuana and two glass vials of cocaine in his jacket. The charge was upped to drug possession. Eric suffered a broken nose in the melée. Later, in a plea bargain, he was found

The two smokers puffed like smokestacks, swore like sailors on shore leave and pursued their frequent arguments at high volumes.

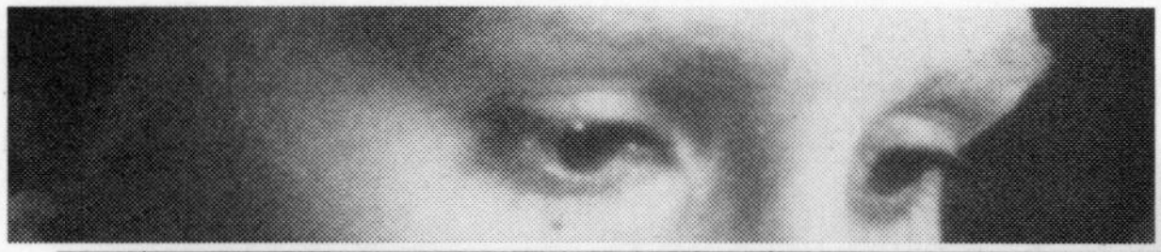

JULIA FAN FACT

Meg Ryan was originally slated to play Shelby Latcherie, the diabetic daughter of Sally Field in the all-star *Steel Magnolias*. But when director Rob Reiner offered Ryan the career-making role of Sally in his new film *When Harry Met Sally*, she dropped out.

guilty on a minor charge of harassment and the drug charges were dropped.

Julia decamped for Liam's digs on the West Coast on May 6, 1988, at which time the world just about lost her. She was feeling tired and worn down but blamed it on her punishing work schedule. When she took a turn for the worse, Liam persuaded her to see a doctor. The physician took one look and rushed his famous patient to the hospital. By the time she arrived she had sunk into delirium and was running a dangerously high temperature. Julia was immediately diagnosed with spinal meningitis. Her mother flew in from Georgia, and even Eric showed up and joined Betty at Julia's bedside, holding back his strong dislike for his mother.

"I thought I was going to die and so did everybody else. So I was forced to face it and found that I wasn't scared to die, that it wasn't a scary thing," Julia said. "Not that I wanted to die, I want to live forever. It's just that having been there, I found out it wasn't such a bad thing."

"I thought I was going to die and so did everybody else. So I was forced to face it and found that I wasn't scared to die, that it wasn't a scary thing," Julia said.

Julia was still recovering when her agents put her up for a part in a *Steel Magnolias*. Her biggest obstacle, however, proved to be the director. Herbert Ross, director of *Funny Lady* and *The Owl and the Pussycat*, wanted a refined southern belle for the role and felt that Julia was too earthy. He watched her well-reviewed turn in *Baja Oklahoma* and came away unimpressed. "She looked bad and gave a very bad performance," he fretted. Ross remained adamant until Sally Field, one of Hollywood's genuinely nice people, personally asked him to audition Julia, whom she had met and liked a few years before. Field even agreed to read with her in the audition.

> Julia, recognizing that this was her chance to move into the big time, gave the reading everything she had. "I had the great fortune of having my audition with Sally," said Julia. "She was great, and she, like, went into this little improv at the end and I was like, 'Whew, here we go,' and we just did the whole thing and it was great."

Ross auditioned 75 other young actresses for the part, working on what seemed to be an "A.B.J." principle—Anyone But Julia. The hard-nosed director put her through five grueling auditions before he gave in and offered her the part.

When she learned she had been chosen to play the

> When she learned she had been chosen to play the doomed Shelby, Julia simply thanked the director. Then she went out and got smashed.

doomed Shelby, Julia simply thanked the director. Then she went out and got smashed.

The actress needed her larger-than-life persona to avoid being swallowed whole by her co-stars. There would be three Academy Award winners in the cast: Field (who had won twice), Shirley MacLaine and Olympia Dukakis. Dolly Parton, Daryl Hannah, Tom Skerritt and Dylan McDermott rounded out the starry list. The producer was Ray Stark, the man behind *The Way We Were* and *Funny Girl.* The budget was set at $35 million.

Ross, ever the martinet, told his budding star that she, already somewhat emaciated after her bout with meningitis, would have to lose weight to play a diabetic, dye her hair a different shade and change the shape of her eyebrows. He gave her a week to do it. Rehearsals in Natchitoches, Louisiana, with four major divas—and Julia Roberts—were about to begin.

And Julia was about to meet a new flame—Dylan McDermott, her rangy, darkly handsome co-star. Romance would flower like the magnolia blossoms that perfumed the drowsy southern air of Natchitoches.

★★★

chapter 4

A Clutch of Divas

There hadn't been such excitement in tiny Natchitoches since John Wayne rode into town to make *The Horse Soldiers* in 1959. Natchitoches is located about 55 miles southeast of Shreveport and is the oldest settlement in Louisiana. The word "sleepy" perfectly describes this picturesque town of 16,000 souls, which slumbers on the banks of the Cane River.

Upon the arrival of the *Steel Magnolias* crew in 1988, "sleepy" went out the window, and the town collectively lost its cool. People hung out in droves at the town's restaurants—there were two of them—in hopes of catching a glimpse of Dolly Parton, Olympia Dukakis, Shirley MacLaine, Daryl Hannah, Sally Field and this new kid, Julia Roberts. They rose early to watch scenes being shot, and they bought *Steel Magnolias* t-shirts on the street corners.

So soon after her own brush with death, Julia joked that the role would be her "first attempt at method acting."

The film's plot was lovingly constructed from the memory of actor/writer Robert Harling. Harling's sister Susan had died of complications from diabetes after giving birth to a baby, a child her doctors had cautioned her against conceiving. *Steel Magnolias* became a long-running off-Broadway hit in which six lively, smart-talking southern women gather at a local beauty salon for gossip and moral support.

Sally Field had nabbed the central role of M'Lynn Eatenton, the mother of Julia's resolute character Shelby. So soon after her own brush with death, Julia joked that the role would be her "first attempt at method acting."

Steel Magnolias (1989)

Hollywood expected that this galaxy of glittering stars would soon go into spectacular meltdown. But the divas actually liked each other, and strong bonds of friendship grew between them. Julia and Sally Field were old friends. Dolly Parton, fresh off her Oscar for writing the hit tune from the movie *9 to 5,* rented a huge home and used it as a retreat where she served home-cooked meals to her co-stars and visiting family members. Daryl Hannah rented a farm, and she and Julia often went riding together. Sally Field, who grew up in the movie industry, was used to the rigors of location shooting. She looked after her infant son Sam and continued to mentor Julia.

Julia needed all the support she could get since Herb Ross stayed on her case throughout the shoot. Ross was an ex-dancer and choreographer and, as Shirley MacLaine observed in her best-selling biography, *My Lucky Stars*: "He regarded Julia as one of his baby ballerinas. That is to say, he wanted to have a ballet master's control over his new discoveries. He wanted (Julia) to have her beauty marks removed and never eat more than 1000 calories in a day. He claimed he could detect the effects of an extra saltine cracker on an actress' face."

According to the others on the set, Julia put everything she had into the role. Ross threw Julia into one of her biggest scenes in the movie—the one in which she has a diabetic fit in the beauty salon—on the first day. Julia still winces at the memory: "I was concentrating so hard on what it would look like inside myself—the way my heart looked, the rate at which it was pumping, all the blood racing through my veins —I got so far down inside my body that as we were coming to the end of the scene, a panic went through me. I had gotten stuck down there and didn't want anybody to know. I thought, 'I'm never going to get out of here!' I finally did, but I sobbed hysterically when it was over."

Robert Harling was riveted. "She came as close to death as

Hollywood expected that this galaxy of glittering stars would soon go into spectacular meltdown. But the divas actually liked each other, and strong bonds of friendship grew between them.

you can while you're still alive," he said. "After every take, they'd have to pick her up and help her back to the trailer. I had been through this sort of thing with my sister, and I just wanted to go over and hug her and tell Herbert, 'Okay, stop it. Let's not do this anymore.'"

But still Ross was unhappy with Julia's performance, and he often chewed her out in front of the crew. At one time, it got so bad that Sally Field told him to stop: "If you don't let up, I'm just going to wait because I can't be around this. It's too pointless, and it's too mean."

> "Are you going back to New York to study acting?" Ross asked Julia.

"What for?" Julia shot back.

But despite the heavy dramatic load, Julia plugged away for her demanding director. In her death scene, she lay in her hospital bed hooked up to IV tubes. She remained still for hours, completely lost in the role. "That created an eerie feeling," remembered a crew member. "You really felt there was a life hovering in the balance, even though we knew it was a set built in a gymnasium. There was an incredible power in her stillness."

Everyone loved the bubbly and self-effacing Dolly Parton, who played Truvy Jones, the salon owner. She explained why the shoot never became "Steel Divas," as was predicted by the tabloids, who anticipated some juicy displays of starry temperament. "I think the reason we all became such good friends is because we all had the same Winnebagos, we didn't have beautiful clothes to fight over and there were no available men."

> "She came as close to death as you can while you're still alive," he said. "After every take, they'd have to pick her up and help her back to the trailer."

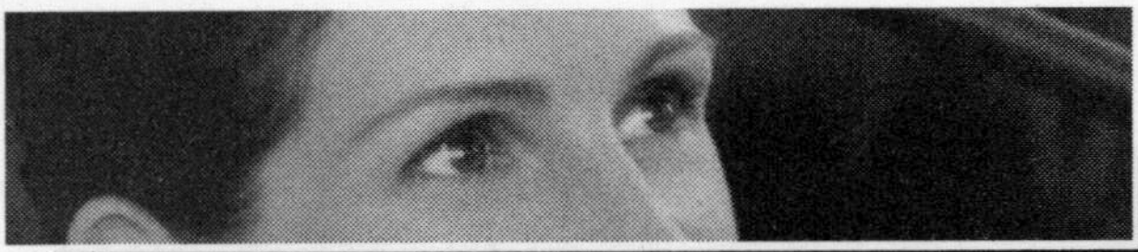

JULIA FAN FACT

After the release of *Steel Magnolias*, Herbert Ross grudgingly admitted that Julia had worked very hard. "She stayed in bed for the coma scenes eight, 12 hours a day, until she was ill and dizzy," he said.

Except one. The character of Jackson Lathery, Shelby's husband-to-be, was played by a tall, handsome and enormously charming actor named Dylan McDermott. The steamy nights in southern Louisiana got a great deal steamier. Julia and Dylan's on-camera relationship spilled over into their private lives, and by the time the shoot ended in September 1988, the two were engaged.

Liam Neeson, who guards his privacy zealously, has never spoken to the press about the breakup, but apparently he was devastated. Friends report that it took him a long time to get over it. Julia has commented that she felt badly about her sudden change of heart. She was quoted as saying: "I adored him as a person and admired him tremendously as an actor. I have only fond memories of Liam. I know I hurt him, and I'm sorry."

However, it was not the last time Liam Neeson was to play a role in the young star's life.

Julia and Dylan's on-camera relationship spilled over into their private lives, and by the time the shoot ended in September 1988, the two were engaged.

On its release in November 1989, *Steel Magnolias* met with generally upbeat reviews. *Rolling Stone*'s Peter Travers noted: "This laugh-getting, tear-jerking, part affecting, part appalling display of audience manipulation is practically critic-proof. The result can be described as shamelessly entertaining."

In *Newsweek*, David Denby took special note of Julia's performance, effusing: "(She) lights up the screen with her liquid fire." The Academy Award jury also noted her efforts and nominated her for an Oscar.

> **Despite the frequent use of that kiss-of-death phrase "chick flick," audiences (indeed, mostly women) stood in line to see *Steel Magnolias*. It finally spun the turnstiles to the tune of $90 million.**

Julia saw herself on an upward trajectory towards superstardom. But she didn't think she could do it with her current management. Back when Julia was being considered for *Satisfaction*, her manager, Bob McGowan, had phoned the William Morris Agency looking for an agent for his nascent star (by law, managers are not allowed to negotiate for their clients). He contacted agent Risa Shapiro, who said she wasn't interested. But when he mentioned that *Satisfaction* was being produced by television mega-producer Aaron Spelling and might lead to a series, the mighty agency quickly came on board. Julia's career was thereafter handled by two agents: Elaine Goldsmith and the reluctant Risa Shapiro. Neither one wanted their new client.

Bob McGowan still speaks of the events that followed *Steel Magnolias* with some pain. After navigating the embryonic actress through the financial and emotional reefs of her early years, she fired him. A worried McGowan came to Julia after the release of *Steel Magnolias* and asked,

Julia's career was thereafter handled by two agents: Elaine Goldsmith and the reluctant Risa Shapiro. Neither one wanted their new client.

"Julia, what's going on with you? Are we going to work together or not?"

She hugged him and replied, "Bob you started all this. I want you in my life forever." Ten days later he received a phone call from Julia's new manager, Elaine Goldsmith, telling him he was fired.

Julia hasn't talked to McGowan since, although she did tell an interviewer: "That was the first completely difficult decision I had to make in my life. Bob had gone to bat for me, but I had to be honest. We'd outgrown each other. There were too many people around me making decisions, and I wanted a clearer line between me and the work. I'm the show, Elaine and Risa are the business. They take care of the stuff I'm not meant to deal with. If it concerns me, they let me know."

After *Steel Magnolias,* Julia was in the position to turn down many of the scripts sent to her. She was interested in one that seemed to allow her to spread her thespian wings. Written by J.F. Lawson, the film was entitled *3000* and told the gritty story of a drug-addicted prostitute who meets a wealthy corporate raider who offers her $3000 (hence the title) to spend a week with him as an escort for a number of social obligations. In the whirlwind week, he shows the woman a world of glamour and excess she has never experienced before. After a week, he drops her off at the same corner where he picked her up.

Julia Roberts loved the project but had to overcome Disney's objections to her scruffy personal image. Could this neo–bag lady manage the transformation from street hooker to glamorous escort?

The film was a project of the family-friendly Disney corporation, of all people.

But the script was, in industry terms, "Disney-fied." Michelle Pfeiffer received the first offer for the role, and she passed.

Al Pacino, Sean Connery and even the singer Sting were all considered for the role of Edward Lewis, the rapacious corporate raider. They all turned it down. It then turned up on the desk of Richard Gere, who looked at it sourly. He later commented, "It was not the kind of movie that I do. In this film, the exotic flower was the girl. Usually, I'm the exotic flower."

Julia Roberts loved the project but had to overcome Disney's objections to her scruffy personal image. Could this neo–bag lady manage the transformation from street hooker to glamorous escort? *Steel Magnolias* hadn't been released yet, and despite her growing resumé, Julia had yet to prove that she could open a picture or attract a substantial audience on the power of her name alone.

The developing script and the developing star circled each other like in celestial bodies in the firmament. Soon they would come together in a supernova that would create one of Hollywood's great stars and change the course of the movies.

★★★

chapter 5

pretty is as pretty Does

Julia Roberts desperately wanted to play Hollywood hooker Vivian Ward. The script for *3000* had changed greatly from the dark original and morphed into a charming fable in which a feisty, likeable Cinderella ends up with a fabulous wardrobe, a lot of expensive jewelry and a rich Prince Charming.

Director Garry Marshall (*Laverne and Shirley, Beaches*) had signed on to direct. Disney was still not sure about Julia, so her agents went into overdrive. Elaine Goldsmith made sure that Disney CEO Michael Eisner and a group of his top lieutenants watched *Mystic Pizza* and *Steel Magnolias*. Observed David Hoberman, the president of Disney's Touchstone Pictures: "Elaine was like a dog tugging at your cuff who wouldn't let go." At Goldsmith's urging, Sally Field phoned Eisner to champion Julia's abilities. Auditions were arranged. Marshall sent Gere a copy of *Mystic Pizza*, but the actor continued to drag his feet, so Marshall and Roberts flew to the actor's lavish Greenwich Village apartment to meet him in person. He was impressed.

It took Julia and her army of supporters a year to storm the breaches, but Disney finally gave in to their unrelenting force. Julia hadn't worked at anything else during that year, and she was ecstatic at the news. She immediately phoned her mother, then realized that she had to tell her that was she going to play a whore in a movie. Julia recalled: "My mom works for the Catholic Archdiocese of Atlanta. I mean, my mom's boss baptized me. So I called her at work, and it was like, 'Hi, Mom. I got a job.' She said, 'You did? What did you get?' And I said, 'Oh it's a Disney movie. I gotta go, Mom. I'll talk to you later.'"

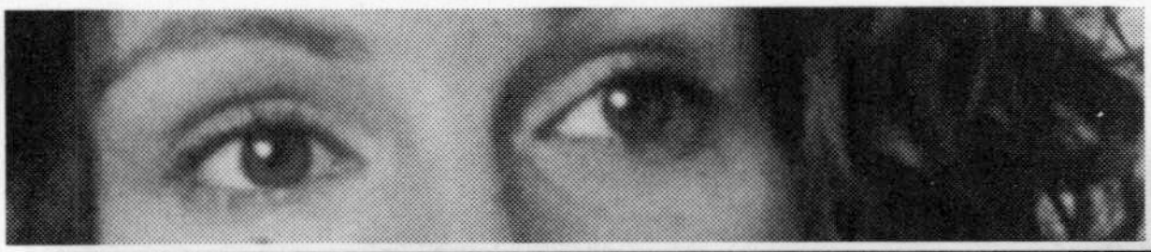

JULIA FAN FACT

One of the scenes that many people remember from *Pretty Woman* was the result of director Garry Marshall's effort to push Julia beyond herself. In this scene, Edward (Richard Gere) gives Viv a box containing a sparkling diamond necklace. Without telling Julia, Marshall told Gere to snap the box shut just as Julia reached for it. The snap surprised the actress who let out her trademark shriek followed by that unique, glass-shattering horselaugh. The true Julia shone through, and Marshall kept the scene in the finished film.

Despite the bizarre circus of her family's at-home relationships, Julia had a fairly normal upbringing. As a Catholic schoolgirl, she certainly knew little about hookers, upscale or otherwise. So she hung out with the working girls for a while. Now there's an image for you to savor—the future America's Sweetheart taking streetwalkers out for burritos at lunch. Julia found it a dismaying and melancholy experience. These young girls had the same hopes and dreams as any women their age, yet they were living dead-end lives.

Julia made use of her experiences on the street when filming started on July 24, 1989. "A lot of it was improvisational," she recalled. "I would just say things that I knew, and Garry let me do that." Julia felt she had a fix on the way Viv felt, and even the way she moved. "That was sort of the beginning of thinking I was in control of this girl—that I found her voice and what made her funny and silly."

Pretty Woman (1990)

Marshall insisted on shooting in a real red-light district. "I know how to deal with any kind of attention anyone is going to give Julia Roberts," she griped afterward. "But the attention that Julia got as Vivian, standing on Hollywood Boulevard in that outfit, was not the kind of attention I am used to or prepared to deal with. At one point, there were so many catcalls, I went back to my trailer and felt hideous. I just wanted to hide. Vivian would say, 'F*** you! Blow it out your ass!' to anyone who barked at her. I turn red and get hives."

Another issue involved nude scenes. Julia simply didn't want to take her clothes off for the camera. But at that time, she didn't have any clout in Hollywood, and the nude scenes stayed in. But Marshall worked out a compromise. Julia performed the bubble bath scene in her bathing suit, and then Marshall pulled everyone, including the cameraman, out of the room. With the camera still running, Julia—all alone—took off the suit beneath the bubbles and climbed out of the tub. "There was nothing in front of me except a camera lens," chortled Julia. "It was quite funny."

It didn't take Marshall long to realize that his star was high-maintenance. Marshall is a gregarious, cheerful man with a great sense of humor that dates the way back to the days when he wrote jokes for Joey Bishop and Dick Van Dyke. He took to calling Julia "Bambi" on the set. "Julia needs a lot of holding and hugging," he wrote. "Particularly in scenes where there's meanness. In the scenes where she got beat up by Richard's lawyer and when Richard screamed at her, she was playing the vulnerability off-camera, so she could play against it on-camera. So off-camera I had a sobbing mess on my hands." If a scene proved too much for her, she'd plaintively request that the director "hug the schlumpy girl."

> "Julia needs a lot of holding and hugging," he wrote. "Particularly in scenes where there's meanness."

Gere, who is not only one of Hollywood's beautiful people but an almost overwhelming charismatic presence in person, also helped. Julia liked her co-star. In fact, she developed something of a crush on him.

She later commented to *People* magazine: "He stayed at the low end in performance terms, which is unique in talented people. He made Vivian an interesting character by making Edward show that he found her interesting—otherwise, she'd just seem like a wacko. He did it for me. He gave me the opportunities even when it meant he, himself, was standing back. He is an incredibly generous actor."

Perhaps she liked him a bit too much. In her own supersized way, she enthusiastically hugged and kissed her co-star off-camera and generally gave the impression of being infatuated. The media immediately picked up on the story and it escalated into an affair—disquieting news for Dylan McDermott, who was filming in Morocco. McDermott flew secretly to Los Angeles, showed up at the set and did not like what he saw. Richard and Julia obviously had something going on. Richard treated her tenderly, exploiting the actress' infatuation with him to make their scenes work. Julia was as flighty as a schoolgirl on her first date, with no idea that McDermott was lurking in the shadows, watching. When the scene was over, he confronted Julia, and their relationship began its slow course to dissolution, although it's not quite clear if it ended because of McDermott's jealousy or whether it had just run out of steam.

Wrote syndicated columnist Liz Smith: "They (Julia and McDermott) started having a wild affair and seemed to be very, very much in love. Julia was very sweet to him—very into him. Then all of a sudden, she dumped him. Her time limit seems to be 12 to 18 months. As soon as the romance gets serious, she can't handle it. She can't seem to handle the reality of commitment."

> "As soon as the romance gets serious, she can't handle it. She can't seem to handle the reality of commitment."

Other events followed that must have shaken Julia's already precarious self-image. Rumors of a body double began to surface, and these rumors turned into a mini-firestorm after the film exploded into a box office phenomenon. Suddenly everyone became fascinated by the minutia of Julia Robert's life. Despite dutifully reported stories to the contrary, Marshall maintains that the body we see in the slow, luxurious pan in the opening shot in the film was indeed Julia's but, for inexplicable reasons, a body double named Donna Scoggins was featured in the famous print poster.

Pretty Woman slipped into theaters on March 23, 1990. The film grossed $11 million on its opening weekend—respectable but not spectacular and giving no indication of the dizzying heights to which it would climb. Some critics attempted to swipe at the film but, like *Steel Magnolias,* it proved critic-proof. Those that did like it were wildly enthusiastic. Said Roger Ebert in the *Chicago Sun Times*: "The sweetest, most openhearted love fable since *The Princess Bride.* The *Washington Post* burbled: "…seduces all but the most wary." Thanks to word of mouth and the press frenzy over the emergence of the first big female star since Barbra Streisand, *Pretty Woman* began its ascent up the box office ladder and into the hearts of film patrons everywhere. It became the fourth highest-grossing movie of the year behind *Home Alone, Ghost* and *Dances With Wolves.* Even overseas audiences who flocked to Bruce Willis and Arnold Schwarzenegger action flicks embraced this sunny story filled with laughter and love. Offshore box offices contributed an awesome $280 million to the film's coffers.

Pretty Woman also changed Hollywood's attitude towards female stars. During the '30s and '40s, strong female like Bette Davis and Barbara Stanwick were powerful box office magnets. But as the movie audience grew younger and adolescent boys began to rule at

***Pretty Woman* also changed Hollywood's attitude towards female stars.**

the ticket wicket, American films skewed more and more to big explosions, car chases and gunfights. These testosterone-drenched, violence-oriented films also traveled well. Light comedies like *Pretty Woman* were regarded as telling stories only of interest to the American culture. Willis and Schwarzenegger were able to pull down paychecks in excess of $10 million because, even if their films didn't do well at home, they made millions abroad. Their female co-stars were paid in the $1 million range. Julia Roberts changed all that with one movie. Millions of people worldwide lined up to see this vivacious new star.

Everyone now wanted Julia Roberts in their movies and were willing to pay for the honor. Elaine Goldsmith jacked the actress' salary up to $3 million for her next film, *Dying Young*.

Julia herself didn't know any of this—she was off shooting on a set far away from the seat of Hollywood power politics.

★★★

chapter 6

Giving All for the Art

The first time director Joel Schumacher saw Julia Roberts, he was struck by her beauty: "I was sitting by the pool when Julia came bouncing over. She was wearing cutoff jeans and a little t-shirt, was barefoot and had no makeup, and all that gorgeous red hair was piled in pins on top of her head. She was one of the most beautiful women I had ever seen, and she had no idea how beautiful she was." His latest project, a film called *Flatliners*, told the story of a group of medical students who experimented in stopping their hearts for short periods of time to experience death. The film wandered from sci-fi into horror when the explorers who have "flatlined" discover people from their guilty pasts who follow them back into life with lethal intent. Schumacher, an intense but gregarious fellow who made his name with such films as *St. Elmo's Fire* and *The Lost Boys*, was smitten. He chose Julia to star as Rachel, one of the daring students. Her co-stars were to be Oliver Platt, William Baldwin, Kiefer Sutherland and Kevin Bacon.

Julia flew to Chicago, where the film was being shot, less than a week after *3000* (yet to be named *Pretty Woman*) wrapped. She met Kiefer Sutherland her first day on set.

In 1989, Kiefer Sutherland was one of Hollywood's hot young stars. His insolent good looks, bad-boy reputation and onscreen intensity had already had an impact on young fans.

Julia and Joel Schumacher proved to be kindred souls and bonded on the set, but it was Kiefer that set fire to her passions. At the time, Kiefer

"Kiefer was unlike anyone I had ever met before. There's something about him that is incredibly old and wise."

maintained that he had not seen any of Julia's films: "I had no reason to like or dislike this person. There was no outside input except for my agent saying, 'Oh, I'm so glad Julia Roberts is doing this film.' And I was going, 'Julia who?' and thinking, 'Okay, here's this novice.' Then she came into rehearsal, and she had a really incredible presence, just as a person, which made me sit back and take a look."

He looked, and he liked what he saw. So did she. "I fell for Kiefer the second I laid eyes on him," she said. "We were filming, and he was up to his elbows in blood and gore. I fell in love with him in some of the most gruesome scenes. Kiefer was unlike anyone I had ever met before. There's something about him that is incredibly old and wise. It's staggering to think that he's only a year older than I am. There was this scene we did together in *Flatliners* where he has flatlined, and I'm watching him, and I'm so fascinated by what he was saying that I'd forgotten I had to speak. I got really interested in what was actually happening—he has a profound effect on me."

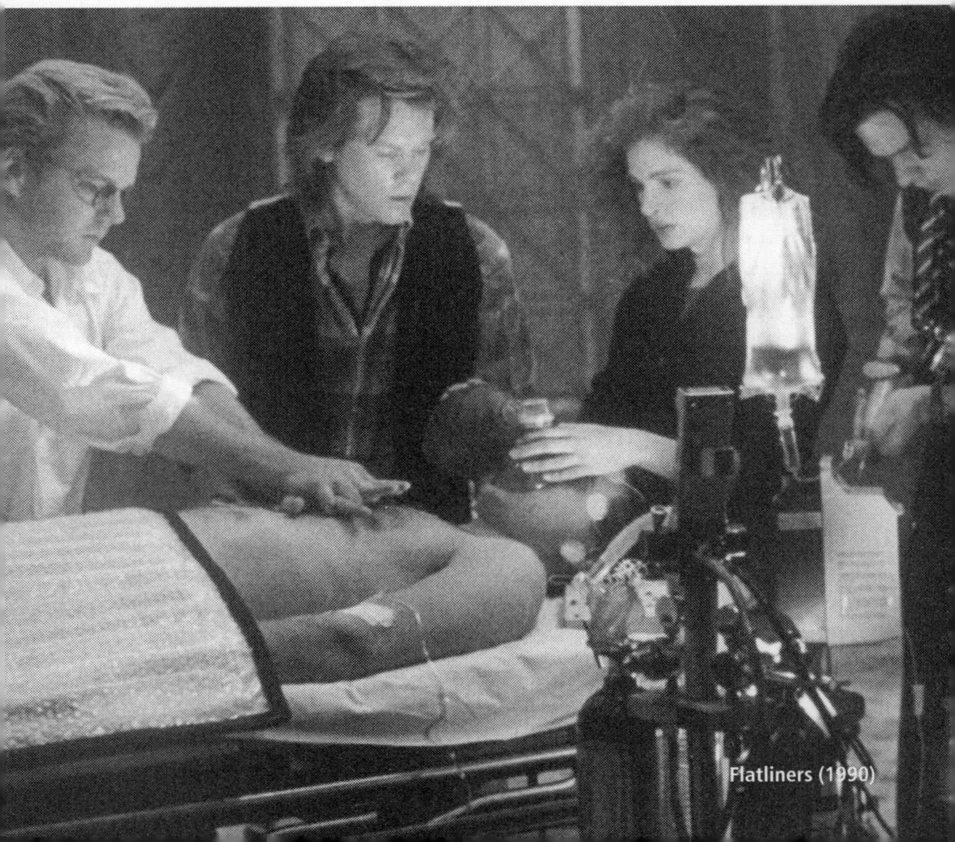
Flatliners (1990)

Julia referred to Kiefer only as "her boyfriend" in a few interviews, because he was still married to his first wife, Camilla Kath, a Puerto Rican actress a decade older than him. The two had an 18-month-old daughter, but their relationship was showing signs of strain even before Kiefer met Julia.

After Kiefer filed for divorce in February 1990, the two secret lovers went public in a big way by attending the Golden Globe Awards together. Although she was only a member of the impressive cast of *Steel Magnolias*, Julia was singled out for a Golden Globe nod. She went on to win. "I almost fell off my f***ing chair," she said. "It was the most shocking night of my life. I was unprepared. I heard a recording of my acceptance speech later. I was such an idiot."

> She said mistily from the podium, "I want to thank my beautiful blue-eyed, brown-eyed boy, who does everything for me." (Kiefer does indeed have different-colored eyes.)

After *Flatliners* wrapped, Julia and Kiefer took off for Tucson, Arizona, where they took time to get to know each other better. Julia, who seldom talks in anything but burnished superlatives about any of her latest loves, cooed: "Kiefer has totally captivated me. Two people couldn't be closer than we are. We've hardly been apart since we met. I've found myself weeping when we're separated. He's so knowledgeable and thinks things through. We sit at home at night reading, or I do a lot of needlework. I've nearly worn a hole in my finger, but that's the kind

> After Kiefer filed for divorce in February 1990, the two secret lovers went public in a big way by attending the Golden Globe Awards together.

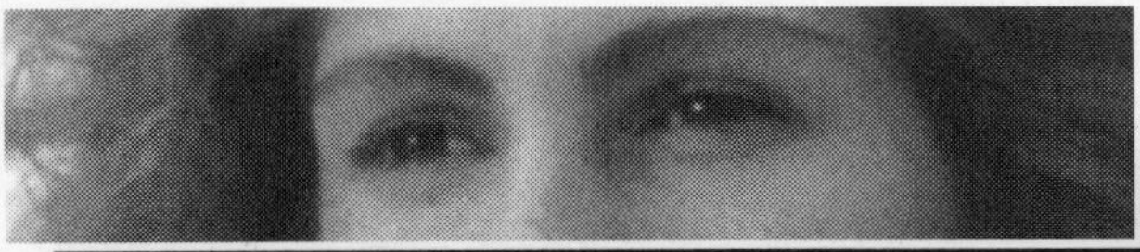

JULIA LOVE-LIFE UPDATE

Two years after the flameout of her grand affair with Kiefer Sutherland, Julia had the tattoo he gave her discreetly removed.

of quiet life we love." He bought her a $100,000 "friendship ring," "without questions and without response," which meant that he had not asked her to marry him. He also paid to have Julia tattooed with a red heart inside a black Chinese symbol, which was supposed to mean "strength of heart." Said Julia: "My love for Kiefer will last as long as this tattoo."

Their idyll together would not last. Soon, he was off to New Mexico to shoot *Young Guns II*, and Julia set out to publicize *Pretty Woman.*

While in Tucson, Julia was nominated for Best Supporting Actress for *Steel Magnolias* by the Academy of Motion Picture Arts and Sciences. "I got a call about five in the morning," recalled Julia. "I was too excited to go to sleep and too tired to get excited. So it was about two in the afternoon, and we'd known since early in the morning, but it just hadn't registered with me. Then, I'm watching MTV, and all of a sudden I stared giggling. I just couldn't stop laughing."

> "It was the most shocking night of my life. I was unprepared. I heard a recording of my acceptance speech later. I was such an idiot."

Julia and Kiefer appeared together again at the Academy Awards in March 1990, where Julia lost to Brenda Fricker for her role as the mother in Daniel Day-Lewis' *My Left Foot.* Shortly after that, Julia left for North Carolina to begin shooting her next film.

Sleeping with the Enemy (1991)

Pretty Woman had just gone into release and the giant wheels of the Hollywood publicity machine were beginning to turn. Julia was touted as "the next big thing."

Her agent Elaine Goldsmith negotiated a $1 million contract for Julia to star in *Sleeping with the Enemy*.

After her tension-filled relationship with Herbert Ross on the set of *Steel Magnolias*, she was in no hurry to put her feet to that fire again. Julia always gives everything she has emotionally on set, and she needs to feel loved and protected. Like many a director before him, *Sleeping with the Enemy*'s Joseph Ruben cherished his star: "I remember this shy but dazzling smile and her body language. It was a shyness, but there was something coming out of her smile. That's the part of what makes her so fascinating onscreen—all the contradictions, being shy, but very much out there are the same time. She's both sexual and very innocent, too. There's an incredibly warm aspect to her, but she can be very cold when she's angry."

As Julia explained to me in an interview shortly before *Sleeping with the Enemy* was released, she would need all the love she could get.

Julia played Laura Burney, the new wife of financial adviser Martin (Patrick Bergin). Laura's seemingly loving husband turns out to be a monster who emotionally and physically abuses her for three long years. One night, to torture her, he insists they go sailing with a neighbor, knowing his wife is a non-swimmer and afraid of the water. However, Laura had learned to swim and fakes her own death. She disappears, but the obsessive Martin later begins to suspect that she is still alive. He tracks her down and begins a series of confrontations that lead to a murder attempt.

"She's both sexual and very innocent, too. There's an incredibly warm aspect to her, but she can be very cold when she's angry."

For Julia, who hates confrontation on either side of the camera, the shoot was long and uncomfortable, and although she got along with

Bergin, the animosity his character showed towards her onscreen began to take a toll. "Every emotion you see in the movie, that you feel or think about from one moment to the next, I probably went through drastically," she told me. "It was physically exhausting. By virtue of size, it was the biggest part I've ever played. And I did get hurt."

Well, yes she did—several times. Although Bergin and his co-star worked out the physical beatings very carefully off-camera (and with such intensity that they unsettled their director), things went very wrong on set. In one highly charged scene, Laura displeases her controlling husband and he slaps her—hard. The slap sent Julia crashing to the floor but she, instinctively, reached out to protect herself. She decided to go for it and fall headfirst into the cushion provided out of camera range. Bergin hit her again, and she spun out of control, missed the pillow and smashed her million-dollar face into the floor. "I really fell, and my head bounced like a basketball on the marble floor. I can't tell you how much that hurt. I'm hysterical with pain. I'm crying. It's gone too far. I cracked the floor so hard I have a black eye, but that's what makes the take so exciting, cracking my head like that."

But the scene was not over. As if some malevolent imp was presiding over the shoot, something even more painful was to come. Bergin was supposed to aim a kick at his wife's prone figure. A sandbag was set up out of frame to absorb his kick, but with the pressures and the tension on the set, Bergin missed the sandbag and kicked his co-star with full force in the stomach. "Anyway," said Julia, blinking in memory of the moment, "I'm in pain and lying there when he kicked me. It can't get any worse. By now I'm a blithering idiot. I can't even see straight.

"I really fell, and my head bounced like a basketball on the marble floor. I can't tell you how much that hurt. I'm hysterical with pain. I'm crying. It's gone too far."

When the take was over, the director came up to me and said, 'I wanted to call CUT! when I saw what happened.' And I said, 'If you'd called CUT! I'd have wrung your neck cause I'm not going to do that scene again.'"

Bergin apologized profusely, but the friendly relationship was over. As Julia observed icily, "We weren't necessarily friendly towards each other. I mean when you come to work, and somebody kicks the sh** out of you for three hours, you don't feel like finding out where he is and saying 'Good night.'" This, however, probably benefited the movie—the tension aided in their strained onscreen relationship.

For the scene in which Julia fakes her death, she was to wear only a bra and panties. "It was absolutely freezing," remembered the star. So she, using her newfound diva clout, told the director and crew: "I think we need a little group support here. So drop your trousers. If you're not going to take your pants off, you can stay in the house." Ruben thought the demand was capricious but amusing, so he did. Some of the crew also complied, while others stalked off the set in anger. Julia later rationalized: "It had nothing to do with just getting everybody naked and cold as I was. I think everybody was silently thrilled by it. It was the bonding thing, you know."

Shooting the movie left the actress in distress. Julia told me she liked the finished product, but found the making harrowing. "There were whole weeks where I'd arrive on the set at 5:00 AM, start crying and be the victim of those terrible fights."

> "I think we need a little group support here. So drop your trousers."

The strain spilled out into Julia's offscreen life as well. Unlike Natchitoches, where the southern belle felt right at home, she found little warmth in the town of Abbeville near the studios in

North Carolina. That feeling peaked when she and a black crewman went to a restaurant called Michael's in Abbeville, and the management would not let the man in because of his race.

As they left, Julia bellowed: "You shouldn't call this place Michael's—you should call it 'Bigot's.'" Soon after, she told *Rolling Stone*: "The people were horribly racist and I really had a hard time." The citizens of Abbeville were outraged and took out a quarter page ad in *Variety* and defended themselves under the headline "Pretty Woman? Pretty Low." Julia in turn issued a placating statement saying that she had not mean to tar everyone in Abbeville with the same brush. "I was born in the South, so in no way am I trying to create a stereotype. I was shocked that this type of treatment still exists in America in the '90s—in the South or anywhere else."

> While she was away, trying to cope with her role of abused wife, Julia was fast becoming one of the biggest stars in the world. Kiefer Sutherland would occasionally show up at the shoot and ply her with reports of ***Pretty Woman***'s incredible performance at the box office, but Julia was otherwise engaged and didn't pay much attention.

Her first real inclination of mega-stardom came with the appearance of her first stalker. A young man showed up at the door of her hotel room and tried to be friendly. "I tried to be nice and say, 'That's really nice, see you later,'" shivers the star. But the young man kept coming back until the film posted a policeman outside her door.

Julia returned to Los Angeles pale and wasted. On top of her personal problems, she had to face one of her least-favorite experiences—the junket press interviews at the Four Seasons Hotel. Kiefer was holed up a floor above us because, at the time, the two had no home. The finishing touches were just being added to their new house in Nichols Canyon. Julia spent some time soaking up the sun by the Four Seasons' pool, a magnificent, green-wreathed hideaway overlooking Los Angeles. *People* magazine's current pick as "The Sexiest Man Alive," John F. Kennedy Jr., was also at the pool and the two, according to the magazine, "frolicked" together. *People* went on to report that John's current girlfriend, Daryl Hannah, was told that he was not available for her phone calls while he was at the pool. Kiefer repeatedly called down and received a blow-by-blow description of the poolside antics.

With all this grinding away at her, it was no wonder that Julia acted friendly but a little distant in our interview.

Whatever friction may have developed over the incident was apparently soon forgotten, and Julia and Kiefer moved into their Nicholas Canyon love nest.

Julia may have achieved superstar status, but she was not one to immerse herself in the trappings of traditional Hollywood glamour. Perhaps she felt that her screen image gave her fans enough of that, because she continued to appear in baggy granny dresses or t-shirts and denim overalls. Her magnificent hair often looked as if it had not seen a brush for days. Even at prestigious events, she often chose not to dress up, appearing in her favorite men's suits, usually three or four sizes too large, and hiding her feminine form. Earlier celebrities of the silver screen took great pains to present an almost mystical image in public—they were grand, twinkling stars and never let their fans forget it. When Ava Gardiner, Elizabeth Taylor or Joan Crawford appeared at premieres, the preparations involved were reminiscent of preparations for the taking of Omaha Beach, with designer gowns, fabulous (often borrowed) jewels and hours of makeup. Marilyn Monroe wouldn't go to the supermarket unless

"There are people who see me in a grocery store and think that I should be wearing, like, Chanel or something," Julia once said.

she was in full regalia and makeup. Julia, however, came from a new generation of stars who turned their backs on all that.

"There are people who see me in a grocery store and think that I should be wearing, like, Chanel or something," Julia once said. "They can't respond to the fact that I'm in cutoffs and a t-shirt. As if it's part of my job to always look impeccable. Which isn't ever going to happen. Ever! Or like, when I get off a plane, and people write, 'Darling, find a hairdresser.' It's like, I've been on a plane for 18 hours, sleeping. My skin is sucked dry, my hair is a mess. What do you want from me?"

As a consequence, Julia found herself number one on flamboyant fashion arbiter Mr. Blackwell's Worst Dressed list for 1991.

Julia's life seemed to right itself after her return from *Sleeping With The Enemy. Flatliners* was released to mixed reviews but made far more at the box office than it deserved. The ever-enthusiastic Roger Ebert called it, "an original, intelligent thriller." Everyone agreed that the film's success was mostly because audiences couldn't get enough of the vivacious new star. The fallout over *Pretty Woman* was reaching nuclear proportions. At the height of the frenzy, *Sleeping with the Enemy* was released and to a lukewarm reception by the critics. But with Julia as star, it became a huge hit, grossing more than $100 million.

With her new soul mate, a fast-developing worldwide reputation and the ability to push any film in which she deigned to appear into the box office stratosphere, Julia was queen of the cinematic world.

But heartbreak, the most publicized breakup since the *Titanic* hit that iceberg, and the morning-after feel of failure at the box office waited just around the corner for America's Pretty Woman.

★★★

chapter 7

making life up as you Go Along

Although Julia insisted that she and Kiefer sat at home like characters in a Norman Rockwell painting, in fact the two loved to party. One particular night gained more than a bit of notoriety when it was videotaped by a musician at a party in Maui, Hawaii, in July 1990. The video was subsequently shown on TV's *Inside Edition.* It shows Julia pulling a man's pants down and screaming, "Right on!" Kiefer then splattered her face with chocolate frosting and licked it off. Later, the two engaged in a little "dirty dancing," before Kiefer returned to the bottle of hooch, belched loudly and shouted into the camera, "This is what happens, kids, when you're an alcoholic—you sweat."

Julia was looking for something that would validate her as an actress, and she thought she'd found it in *Dying Young,* the story of nurse Hilary O'Neil, who is hired to care for Victor Gaddes, a rich leukemia victim. Gaddes was to be played by handsome Campbell Scott, the son of Oscar-winner George C. Scott. At Julia's recommendation, the producing company hired her director from *Flatliners,* Joel Schumacher.

When the actress began shooting the film in November 1990, it proved to be more intense than she expected. The melancholy nature of the screenplay, which is pretty well summed up by the title, began to affect her.

When released in June 1991, *Dying Young* didn't click with audiences or critics, and although Julia emoted up a storm, audiences just didn't want to see their pretty woman holding vigil over the bed of a dying man. Martin Grove commented in the *Hollywood*

Dying Young (1991)

Reporter: "They said (Julia Roberts) could open a phone book. *Dying Young* proved they were wrong." Echoed *Time* magazine: "Not even the movies' most reliable female star since Doris Day could peddle leukemia—particularly to a summer audience that only wants the bad guys to die. So *Dying Young* did just that, and Roberts' pristine rep got terminated, too."

Soon, however, Julia's chaotic personal life would eclipse anything she attempted on the screen.

While Julia was shooting *Dying Young* in Mendocino, California, Kiefer was playing househusband in Nichols Canyon. He meticulously arranged their new furniture, hung their clothes in the closets and generally tried to make the place as homey as possible. But the nights were long, and his next film was still some time away.

On the third weekend of February 1991, the tabloid *Globe* hit the stands with the incendiary headline, "Caught! Kiefer 2-Times Pretty Woman Julia Roberts." The article was accompanied by shots of a clearly uncomfortable Kiefer Sutherland with a pretty brunette. The *Globe* article went on to tell of intimate late-night meetings in a restaurant on Sunset Strip. It didn't take the press bloodhounds, hot on the scent of a juicy story, long to come up with a name. The young lady was Amanda Rice, known to her fans as the stripper "Raven" at the Crazy Girls Club on La Brea Avenue. Rice was another pretty young girl who had come to Hollywood with stars in her eyes and took to stripping when movie stardom eluded her. Rice approached the press with the same alacrity she displayed in doffing her clothes. She told one rag that she had heard that Kiefer and Julia were a couple, but "...he told me specifically that he was not engaged. He said they would

"Not even the movies' most reliable female star since Doris Day could peddle leukemia—particularly to a summer audience that only wants the bad guys to die."

not be married, that being with her during the last six months, or so, was hell." As if to kiss his relationship with Julia goodbye, Kiefer took Amanda and their kids to Disneyland. Amanda happily burbled to the press that Sutherland said that Julia was too thin (Rice was indeed a buxom lass), and her skin was too pale. Julia was, she continued, unhappy with her body, and sexually she was a cold fish. Sex with Julia, Kiefer had told her, was like having sex with a corpse. Julia had changed after *Pretty Woman*, trumpeted Amanda Rice. She had become an "ice princess."

Kiefer was thrown out of the Nichols Canyon love nest and went to live in the $105-a-night St. Francis Hotel on Hollywood Boulevard. Hollywood Billiards, a favorite haunt of Amanda's, was across the street from the hotel.

Surprisingly, Julia seemed willing to overlook Keifer's actions. She sent him a note that said: "Remember, there's always a rainbow after the storm." He moved back into their home, and as soon as she finished shooting *Dying Young*, they left to rebuild their relationship at Kiefer's ranch in Whitefish, Montana.

The emotional drain caught up to Julia before long. The wan and painfully thin actress reported to the Cedars-Sinai Medical Center, suffering from a "severe viral infection, headaches and a high fever." The tabloids leaped on the event like starving hounds on carrion, and they immediately blamed Kiefer for her "breakdown." Never letting the facts get in the way of a good story, one tabloid portrayed Julia as a heroin addict going "cold turkey" in the hospital.

Surprisingly, Julia seemed willing to overlook Keifer's actions. She sent him a note that said: "Remember, there's always a rainbow after the storm."

When it was over, Julia spilled her emotions to a reporter: "I was exhausted. I had a fever. A bad fever. That was the worst symptom. It was, like, 104 degrees. That's why I was in the hospital so long. People should be allowed to be sick without

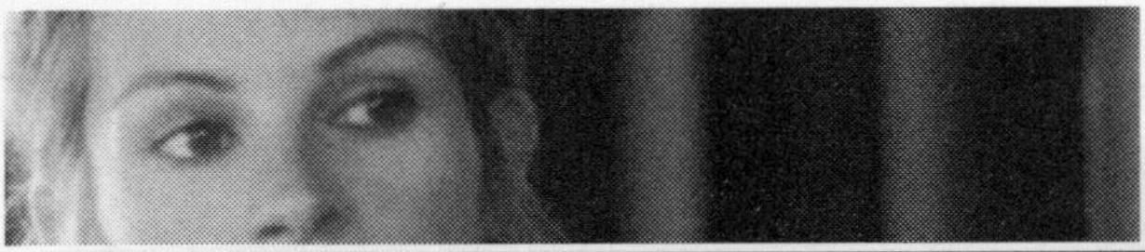

JULIA FAN FACT

Julia's wedding invitees included Emelio Estevez, Sally Field, Michael J. Fox, Richard Gere, Daryl Hannah, Shirley MacLaine, Garry Marshall, Demi Moore, Dolly Parton, Lou Diamond Phillips, Joel Schumacher, Charlie Sheen and Bruce Willis. The cost? An estimated $500,000.

enduring talk that they've got a needle stuck in their arms. I had the flu. I was sick. F*** off."

> At any rate, Julia remained in the hospital for almost a week, with Kiefer at her side the whole time.

Somewhere during all this, Julia and Kiefer became engaged. The bride wanted a small, intimate wedding, but it was not to be. Joe Roth, a long-time friend of Julia's and head of 20th Century Fox, heard of the wedding and decided to pay for it, on his terms. The event was moved to Soundstage 14 on the Fox lot, which would be transformed into a green paradise for the occasion. One hundred and fifty waiters were hired and a huge contingent of security guards set in place to make sure none of the pesky paparazzi sneaked a picture.

Julia was already in town. Kiefer flew in from his ranch in Whitefish, Montana, on June 5. Julia and several friends and family members spent a few days at the exclusive Canyon Ranch Spa in Tucson, and Kiefer's bachelor party took place at Dominick's on Beverly Boulevard, where his cake was a replica of a 15-pound turkey. "Kiefer has a thing for turkeys," reported *People* magazine.

But the event never happened. Early on the morning of June 11, Kiefer got a call from Julia's agent and by now close friend, Elaine Goldsmith, who told him that the wedding was off.

The worldwide reaction was immediate and incendiary. The story leaped out of the entertainment section, vaulted over the gossip columns and made headlines. The two weren't talking, so the press was free to come up with its own conclusions about the cause of the breakup. Some pointed to the stress from Julia's blossoming career and Kiefer's diminishing one. Others suggested that Julia had a secret lesbian lover. Kiefer's out-of-control drinking was cited, as was his affair with Amanda Rice. Some speculated that the wedding was not off at all, but the cancellation was invented as a cover for the real event. That favored source, the "anonymous friend," weighed in with comments like, "The problem was not money or other women. The problem was Julia. Every time she gets close, she just shies away."

Kiefer was apparently heartbroken. He spent the rest of the day trying to phone Julia, who would not take his calls. It was over.

On June 13, the day after the huge wedding scene was disassembled on the Fox lot, Julia posed for photos with Steven Spielberg, the director of her new film *Hook*. She was in a great mood—certainly not the picture of the heartbroken bride. A clue to her happy disposition could be found in the Notre Dame baseball cap she wore for the stills. That team was the particular favorite of the Irish-American actor Jason Patric. After the photos, Julia went directly to Patric's home on Stanley Street in West Hollywood and stayed the night. The next day, which would have been her wedding day, she was seen eating turkey burgers with Patric

"The problem was not money or other women. The problem was Julia. Every time she gets close, she just shies away."

JULIA LOVE-LIFE UPDATE

On June 14, Julia and Jason Patric flew to London and then on to Ireland. They booked into separate rooms at the Shelbourne Hotel in Dublin ($250 a night). Then they went to Eddy Rocket's Diner for burgers.

on Melrose Avenue. (Kiefer spent his wedding day moving his furniture out of the Nichols Canyon house. That night he played pool at Hollywood Billiards.)

The media was a bit baffled by all this but immediately took up the chase. Who was this Patric guy? Well, he was the son of Pulitzer Prize–winning playwright Jason Miller (*That Championship Season*), who also played Father Damien Karras in *The Exorcist.* Patric was known, like Roberts, to have a distinct aversion to, bordering on hatred of, the press. His family was wealthy, but Jason preferred to live like a retro-hippie. His apartment had sheets instead of curtains on the windows and his furniture was other people's castoffs. Professionally, he was known to be difficult and to choose his projects carefully—once he'd gone almost two years without doing a film, turning down all offers because he couldn't find anything he liked.

Julia's take on the whole sorry event with Kiefer came in an interview with *Entertainment Weekly* six months later. She stated that she did not believe Amanda Rice, who had denied ever having a sexual relationship with Kiefer. "I mean, this had been going on for really a long time," said Julia. "So then I had to say, 'Well, I have made an enormous mistake in agreeing to get married. Then I made an even bigger mistake by letting it all get so big. I'm not going to make the final mistake of actually getting married.' At that point I just realized that this had all turned into an enormous joke, and that it wasn't going to be respectable, it wasn't going to be honest, it wasn't going to be simple. And it could have been all those things." Apparently, Rice's disclosure of Julia's physical imperfections and poor body image were too close to reality to have been invented. "Only my wardrobe people know how sick and paranoid I am about this," Julia continued. "With them I go bananas: 'I'm not going to wear that! Let's get one thing straight. These are body parts I have a problem with. These are the ones we will hide, we will conceal, we will make look better. This is your job.'"

Through all her previous woes, Julia had always lost herself in her work, burying herself in the warm family feeling that the movie crews gave her. But even that failed on her next project.

Elaine Goldsmith had landed her a dream contract. Julia would receive $2 million up front (some reports have pegged her up-front salary at $7 million) and a generous back-end deal that would see her production company receive two percent of the film's gross if it went over $100 million. The movie was *Hook,* a retelling of the story of Peter Pan, based on J.M. Barrie's beloved play, except set in the present, with a middle-aged Pan having forgotten what it was like to lead the Lost Boys. The plot involved Peter finding the lost boy within him. Robin Williams took on the role of the grown-up Peter Pan, Dustin Hoffman was slated to play the evil Captain Hook and, everyone's favorite glamorous pixie, Julia Roberts, would flit fearlessly as the seven-inch-tall Tinkerbell. The director? Steven Spielberg.

Through all her previous woes, Julia had always lost herself in her work, burying herself in the warm family feeling that the movie crews gave her.

Spielberg delved into *Hook* with high hopes. A lifelong cinephile, his love of movies is obvious and infectious, and he was particularly happy to be shooting *Hook* on Stage 27 at the Culver City Studios (once the home of fabled MGM), where *The Wizard of Oz* was shot.

But it didn't take long for high hopes to crash into the reality of Hollywood big-budget filmmaking. Tales of expensive set changes and unforeseen costs emerged. The original $56 million budget ballooned into $75 million as Spielberg struggled to keep the unwieldy production under control.

And through it all, Julia's private life was a maelstrom, and it couldn't help but affect her work. She was pale and painfully thin, and upon realizing that she couldn't give the film her best—that she wasn't up to the physical demands of the role—she tried to bail out of her commitment. "I thought it was better to pull out than go in halfhearted and let everyone down," she said.

Despite her sadly accurate forecast, she went ahead anyway. Spielberg wanted her—Tri-Star wanted her—and the monetary rewards were too seductive.

She was right to think that the role would be physically and emotionally demanding. Creating the image of the sprightly pixie who flies effortlessly over London and past "the second star to the right and straight on until morning" was physically taxing and required a lot of harnesses and flying in front of a huge blue screen. She hated the leather-and-chain device that allowed

"I thought it was better to pull out than go in halfhearted and let everyone down," she said.

Hook (1991)

her to fly, calling it "industrial bicycle shorts." Once aloft, she was often dizzy and ill. The frustrated actress spent hours and hours sitting around, waiting for equipment to be set up.

Once when she was really bored, she called out, "I'm ready now." Spielberg reportedly snapped back, "We're ready when I say we're ready, Julia." She didn't even get to work with the other actors. Most of her lines were fed to her by the director.

Tri-Star executives were horrified when they saw none of the sparkle they were expecting. Julia even alienated her last hope for comfort—the crew. She was known for helping out around the set, sitting in on card games, telling dirty jokes and then whooping like a Cherokee warrior. But not on this shoot. Now she was unable to reach out to the crew, and they saw her as "hell to work with." She would often burst into tears for no apparent reason. The crew took to calling her "Tinkerhell."

Rumors of that magnitude couldn't stay on the set and soon leaked out to the press. Reported *USA Today*: "Don't be surprised if Julia Roberts is dropped from Steven Spielberg's in-the-works movie *Hook*." Alternative names began to appear in the press—Annette Bening, Meg Ryan and Michelle Pfeiffer were all mentioned by would-be casting directors.

When the growing rumors began to look as if they might affect the release of the movie, Spielberg and Roberts held an impromptu press conference at the gates of the studio. Spielberg may have been unable or too busy or just unwilling to offer Julia the kind of support she'd gotten from Joel Schumacher or Garry Marshall, but he seemed kind at the portals of old MGM.

> She was known for helping out around the set, sitting in on card games, telling dirty jokes and then whooping like a Cherokee warrior.

"Julia was going through hell at the time for reasons I won't go into," he said. "The last thing she needed to read in the papers was that I was going to fire her. I called a couple of reporters and told them the truth, but the stories kept appearing in print. Coming here says in effect, 'See, we love each other.'"

During this time, Julia put additional stress on her director by taking off for Ireland with Jason Patric. The holiday was well within her contractual obligations, but given her delicate state, Spielberg wasn't sure she would come back. He even went so far as to begin costume fittings for Michelle Pfeiffer. But Julia did return and gamely climbed back into her despised harness. Later, she took a day off to appear in the final scene of the film-within-a-film sequence of Robert Altman's *The Player*, a brilliant exposé of the inner workings of Hollywood. It uses the catchphrase "Julia Roberts would be perfect for this" as a necessary part of every pitch for a movie to be "green-lighted" by a studio. Julia appears at the end of the film as a woman falsely convicted of murder who is rescued at the last moment by Bruce Willis.

> Later, at the press junket for ***Hook*** at the Century Plaza Hotel, she was grumpy and distant. She snapped at one journalist: "You just sort of figure things out as you go along, I guess. I've made plenty of mistakes, and everyone's made sure I've known about them."

The actress was entering a melancholy period, in which those mistakes would begin to pile up, influencing her life and endangering her career.

★★★

chapter 8

Falling Down and Getting Up Again

When it was released in December 1991, *Hook* didn't exactly fly. The star-heavy leviathan made well over $100 million at the box office but not the kind of inflated figures the studio was hoping for. The reviews were almost universally unkind. Said Peter Travers in *Rolling Stone*: "No matter how much cash *Hook* earns, it will take more than pixie dust to fly this overstuffed package into our dreams." Julia was often singled out. Travers went on: "...while Roberts does her best playing a flickering special effect, she's given so little to do that she could be accused of loitering."

When Bradley pressed him further by asking if he would work with her again, Spielberg softly replied, "No!"

But for Julia, the biggest hurt came from Spielberg himself. The highly rated TV magazine *60 Minutes* did a profile of the director on the release of *Hook.* When asked point-blank by interviewer Ed Bradley about the rumors of a rift between himself and Julia, Spielberg attempted to paddle around the rocks by observing, "It was not a great time for Julia and I to be working together." When Bradley pressed him further by asking if he would work with her again, Spielberg softly replied, "No!"

Julia told *Premiere Magazine* that she almost burst into tears when she saw the interview. As she remembered it: "Steven and I had an enjoyable time...To have him even say that it was difficult for me to be going through a personal experience like that while making a movie—well, yeah, it is. Do I

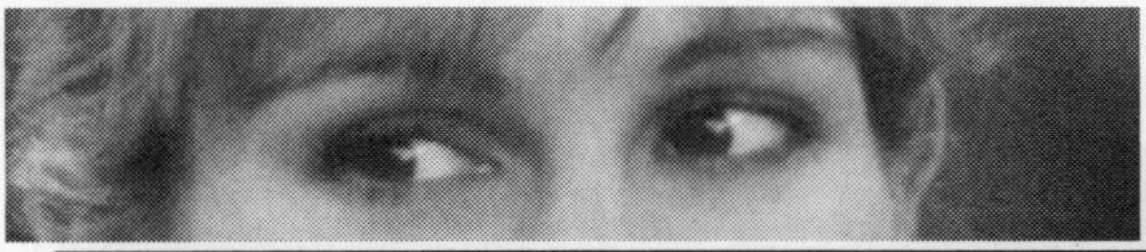

JULIA FAN FACT

By 1992, rumors of Julia's drug abuse had grown so prevalent that in an interview with *Entertainment Weekly*, she bared her arms showing that they bore no needle marks. She told the magazine: "People walk in with these preconceived notions and these rumors in their heads. You just can 't win with these people. It's just silly. The fact is that I don't use, nor have I ever used, drugs."

feel like I inconvenienced him with my personal life in any way, shape or form on the set? No."

And with that, Julia turned her back on Hollywood.

The star went into a seclusion that lasted for two years—a hiatus that could very well have ended her film career. During that sabbatical, she surfaced from time to time in the tabloids but then disappeared again. In December 1991, she accompanied Jason Patric to the premiere of his film *Rush*. She made several visits back home to Smyrna. She even trekked to India to spend two weeks in one of Mother Teresa's missions for children. She began to appear less and less often in public with Patric. In September 1992, she and her lover attended an MTV concert by Bruce Springsteen. After the show, Julia was deep in a conversation with Bon Jovi guitarist (and lover of high-profile stars like Cher), Richie Sambora. Patric got bored and began to throw pieces of licorice at her to get her attention. She ignored him. The actor finally came over and took her hand to pull her away. She drew back and glared at him, spitting out, "You don't own me!" Patric withdrew and stood by uncomfortably until Julia was finished.

During her self-imposed exile, Julia turned down a number of juicy roles, including a co-starring turn with Tom Hanks in *Sleepless in Seattle* and a role opposite Robert Redford in *Indecent Proposal.* She also flirted with the lead in *Shakespeare in Love,* opposite Daniel Day-Lewis (with whom she reportedly had a dalliance), but when he pulled out so did she. Gwyneth Paltrow inherited the role and went on to win an Academy Award. It might have been interesting to see what Julia would have done with it. Professionally, she was just coming off a flop (*Dying Young*) and a perceived failure (*Hook*). One Hollywood producer commented: "It's not that the bloom is off Julia Roberts, it's just that she's going to have to gain momentum again. Hollywood is really a town of who is the flavor of the month. With each passing month there is less and less demand for her services. I still think of her as bankable. But how long are the studios going to risk huge budgets on an unproven?"

People magazine may have headlined "Whatever Happened to Julia Roberts?" but in 1991, she was on the cover of more magazines than any other person.

What the doom-spouting Cassandras did not take into consideration was the genuine affection Julia had generated in the hearts of her millions of fans. To them, no matter her professional missteps and personal gaffs, she would always be the vivacious Vivian Ward of *Pretty Woman,* pulling herself up from the streets of Hollywood by sheer personality and style to become a woman of glamour and riches. They remembered that mile-wide smile and the infectious love of life that lit up the screen and their hearts. Ask anyone what movie they remember Julia Roberts for—it is inevitably *Pretty Woman,* even after all these years.

People magazine may have headlined "Whatever Happened to Julia Roberts?" but in 1991, she was on the cover of more magazines than any other person.

Over the years, Julia has often remarked that she

doesn't care much for the star system and that the grosses of her last film don't interest her as much as the work. She is able to say that because *Pretty Woman* banked an almost inexhaustible supply of good will and fan support. That account has left her with an abundant investment of built-up devotion.

Julia's on-again/off-again affair with Jason Patric ended in a spectacular flameout. On January 18, 1993, Patric's neighbors were awakened by angry voices in the night. As they recounted it later to the press, his door flew open, and the two catapulted into the street. Apparently the argument was based on her fling with Daniel Day-Lewis. One witness reported that Patric was almost "falling down drunk," and Julia wasn't far behind.

He kept accusing her of sleeping with the English actor, yelling, "You f****d him. I know you f****d him." Julia shot back, "I can f*** anybody I want to." She then jumped into her car and sped away, out of Patric's life.

"Rusty? I don't feel rusty. Do I look rusty? I think I came back with renewed vigor…I've been giddy." These are the words of Julia Roberts to a press conference to promote her new film *The Pelican Brief*, on June 17, 1993. "Maybe the press will focus on the work instead of me and how many times a week I do my laundry," she added hopefully.

Her co-star Denzel Washington then asked meekly, "So how many times a week do you do your laundry?"

Denzel was present at Julia's insistence. The character he played was white in John Grisham's original novel, but Julia felt that the black actor, who won a Best Supporting actor Oscar for 1989's *Glory*, would bring the right gravitas to the role. Grisham's bestselling legal thriller depicted Roberts as Darby Shaw, an obscure Tulane law student who writes a paper with a supposition as to why the justices of the American Supreme Court are

Over the years, Julia has often remarked that she doesn't care much for the star system and that the grosses of her last film don't interest her as much as the work.

The Pelican Brief (1993)

being systematically murdered. Her theory proves correct, and her life becomes endangered by dark forces seeking to subvert the American legal system. When her professor is killed by a car bomb meant for her, she enlists Gray Grantham (Washington), an investigative reporter, to help her.

> The warmth of a New York summer's morning was spreading over Manhattan when Julia Roberts stepped onto a movie set for the first time in two years in early June 1993. "I feel ready to blow the door open," Julia told ***Variety.*** Her $8 million paycheck, the highest ever paid to a female performer, probably helped her feeling of elation.

But perhaps her outward enthusiasm was more than a little whistling in the dark. Later she admitted, "I hadn't worked in two years, and I truly got to that set and I thought, 'What if I've forgotten how to act? What if they say ACTION! And I just stand there?'" Her director, Alan J. Pacula (*All the President's Men*, *Sophie's Choice*), wasn't worried about the tales of Steven Spielberg's trials with Julia. He gave his unsure star the kind of emotional and professional support she needed.

The Pelican Brief proved to be a pleasant shoot for all, although Julia did experience a couple of frightening events during that time. She began to receive love letters from a male fan. There was nothing new in that, but these letters turned nasty and threatening. At about the same time, the actress was walking to a nearby coffee shop during a break in the shooting when somebody suddenly recognized her. Soon she was mobbed by frenzied fans and the crush of people began to suffocate her.

"All that kept going through my mind was that the man who's after me could be in this crowd. I didn't dare focus on anyone. I just kept pleading, 'Please, move back. Please give me room to breathe. You're scaring me.'" A passing patrolman scattered the crowd, but Julia was always accompanied by a plainclothes security guard from then on.

And yet again, Julia's personal life took an unexpected and headline-grabbing turn. She met and married Lyle Lovett, the gangly country balladeer with the craggy face and towering hairstyle (described by *People* magazine as "a thatch of nuclear-radiated alfalfa sprouts").

At first, Julia denied the rumors of her interest in Lovett, and even commented to a reporter with a straight face: "That's funny…I mean, I do *know* Lyle. He played here in D.C. and a whole bunch of us went. We went on this big bus because there were about 25 of us from the crew." Everyone believed her. After all, Julia Roberts could have her pick of the best-looking men in the world—why would she choose a country singer with a face like a road map?

Some observers pointed out that in all the beauty and the beast controversy, Julia Roberts had done all right for herself. She had landed a charming, highly intelligent and creative artist who had his feet in the good Texas dirt and his head in a creative world of ideas, words and music. And he loved her very much.

A week later, *Time* magazine had the scoop. Pretty Woman and the rugged singer/songwriter/actor had married.

Lovett had been a fan of Julia's for some time, and she often played his music in her motor home while shooting. In fact, she had every recording he had ever made. During an afternoon TV chat show, the host had asked Julia to name her favorite country singer, and she said, "Lyle Lovett." The Grammy Award–winning singer was watching and was pleasantly

At eight o'clock that evening, in the Deer Park Amphitheater, Julia walked onstage and announced to the world: "Ladies and gentlemen, my husband…Lyle Lovett."

surprised. He was on the road promoting his new release, *Joshua Judges Ruth,* when a friend told him how much Julia enjoyed his work, and he plucked up the courage to phone her. Both Lyle and Julia had appeared in Altman's *The Player,* but their scenes were shot on different days.

The two met for the first time on June 8, 1993, in New Orleans where Julia was shooting *The Pelican Brief.* Julia wore a simple cotton dress and no makeup or shoes. They hit it off immediately. She began to show up at his concerts, and he would dedicate songs to Fiona (Julia's middle name). On June 22, during a concert at the Paramount Theatre in New York, he said from the stage, "I love you, Fiona." Five days later they were married in Marion, Indiana, after collecting their marriage license at the County Clerk's office. The church was decorated with small bouquets of purple, red and yellow flowers. Julia's mother Betty was there, as was her half-sister Nancy. The chief bridesmaid was Lisa Roberts, and the other bridesmaids were Elaine Goldsmith, actress Deborah Goodrich, long-time friend Susan Sarandon and Paige Sampson, Julia's closest friend from Campbell High School in Smyrna. Julia went barefoot, and the groom wore a dark suit. Halfway through the ceremony Julia was overcome and burst into tears, followed closely by Lovett. The entire ceremony took about 20 minutes. A soft rain began to fall as they left the church.

At eight o'clock that evening, in the Deer Park Amphitheater, Julia walked onstage and announced to the world: "Ladies and gentlemen, my husband... Lyle Lovett." Ten thousand fans gave them a rapturous ovation.

Julia summed up the whirlwind courtship like this: "It's funny. We were both just giddy and wanted to get together and get married. Certainly as an afterthought, you go 'Let's do it now!' We love each other. We want to spend our lives together."

Her brother Eric was notably not invited. His erratic behavior continued, and Julia had obviously turned away from him. Early that year, he had split up with his girlfriend, Kelly Cunningham, and had publicly fought for the custody of their daughter, Emma. Julia had coldly taken Cunningham's side in the fracas, which, not surprisingly, infuriated Eric. Eric and Lyle have never met.

At the same time, Julia's press representative, Nancy Seltzer, was having a hard time convincing the press that the couple had gotten married. She rang up Associated Press with the good news, and no one would believe her: "I could not prove to them who I was," she protested. "The AP asked me to name my clients, so I did. Then I said, 'What about Julia's agent Elaine Goldsmith? She's right here.' But then she couldn't prove who she was either. In the end, Susan Sarandon came on the phone and spoke to several people at AP before the news agency finally decided to put the story on the wire."

Two days later, the now-famous couple separated for the first time. He went on to his concert dates, and she flew to New Orleans to finish *The Pelican Brief.* On breaks in the filming and after the shoot was over, Julia took to appearing with Lyle at his concerts and singing with him onstage.

The *Globe* tabloid scooped the world with the first pictures. Well, actually they were publicity shots from Julia's screen wedding to Dylan McDermott in *Steel Magnolias.* The editors simply snipped off the actor's head and replaced it with Lyle's.

The Pelican Brief opened on December 17, 1993, and Julia Roberts was back. Roger Ebert rhapsodized: "Julia Roberts, returning after two years off the screen, makes a wonderful heroine—warm, courageous, very beautiful. Denzel Washington shows again how credible he seems on the screen—like Spencer Tracy he can make you believe in almost

> ...despite the public's obvious love of the movie star and her good ol' boy country singer husband, distance, time and new romances doomed their relationship.

any character." *Variety* approved, noting that the film was "a crackling thriller." The movie-going public had obviously forgiven Julia for *Hook* and *Dying Young* and lined up around the block. *The Pelican Brief* made almost $159 million domestically and $140 million more in international ticket sales.

Julia went **immediately** onto her next film, a **supposedly** **lighthearted caper flick** called ***I Love Trouble.*** Lyle was **performing** every night somewhere else.

The euphoria of *The Pelican Brief* was short-lived however. The weak title of *I Love Trouble* reflected the rest of this uncomfortable, problem-plagued film, and despite the public's obvious love of the movie star and her good ol' boy country singer husband, distance, time and new romances doomed their relationship. Julia Roberts was once again headed for professional uncertainty and personal grief.

★★★

chapter 9

drifting Apart

For 20 years, Nick Nolte has been Hollywood's bad boy. He is a notoriously bellicose drunk, and I have left late-night parties when things turned nasty, with Nolte at the center of it.

I have interviewed the actor on several occasions while he was wearing hospital sweats. When I asked him why, he was up front about it: "I wear them to remind myself that I am just a step away from incarceration in a mental ward." Early in October 2002, Nolte *was* incarcerated when he was picked up in Malibu and charged with driving under the influence of drugs and alcohol. The now-famous mug shot quickly flashed all over the world, and the actor was later to term the event "a call for help." Apparently the green hospital sweats weren't enough.

Nolte is also a huge presence—he fills a room. He is a very able, intelligent actor and capable of great charm, when he cares to use it. After a respectful period of time after the June 1994 release of their film *I Love Trouble*, Julia said: "From the moment I met him, we sort of gave each other a hard time, and naturally we got on each other's nerves. While he can be completely charming and very nice, he's also completely disgusting. He's going to hate me for saying this, but he seems to go out of his way to repel people."

I Love Trouble was meant to be a frisky romantic comedy about two competing Chicago journalists, made in the light-hearted style and with the snappy patter of a Spencer Tracy–Katherine Hepburn film. The writer/director was Charles Shyer, responsible for *Father of the Bride* and *Baby Boom.*

Hopes were high. "Julia Roberts in a romantic comedy. I think it might work," chuckled producer Joe Roth. Everyone's (including Julia's) first choice as co-star was Harrison Ford, but Ford turned it down. So the producers offered the role to Nolte, who snapped it up.

In the film, Julia plays Sabrina Peterson, a green but eager young reporter trying to establish herself in the world of Chicago journalism. Nolte plays hard-drinking Peter Brackett, a crusty, womanizing columnist and king of the Chicago newspaper scene. Both work for competing newspapers and find themselves assigned to cover the same story: a train wreck. He offers tips and advice, she scoops him, then he gets even. But the two are forced to work together when they discover that some shady scientists at a chemical company have developed a new kind of milk—one that causes cancer—and are hushing it up.

The hope for any kind of onscreen (or offscreen) rapport between the two stars disappeared very quickly. Nolte made no effort to clean up his act for his young co-star, and Julia made no secret that she found him a boor. When the lack of chemistry

I Love Trouble (1994)

between the actors became obvious in the daily rushes, the marketing department changed the campaign. Instead of a feel-good summer comedy, *I Love Trouble* was now a murder mystery.

"If you read the script, you'd know why I did the film," Julia posited. "It was clever banter, '40s-style, hard driving, a little wacky, a little screwball, a little adventure. But throughout the making of the movie, these things weren't supported by our leaders. It became a '90s movie that didn't know what it was."

The film was released in June 1994 and immediately misfired at the box office. Internet reviewer Frank Ochieng summed up the general critical reaction when he found it "disjointed and tedious, featuring the miscast leads of Nolte and Roberts who toil along in this dull and draining ditty." Julia termed the film "a disaster."

You couldn't call the end of Julia's marriage to Lyle Lovett a disaster because that sounds too immediate and catastrophic. The two simply drifted apart as their careers carried them to different parts of the globe. Perhaps the early warning bells were already sounding on their wedding night. Instead of a cozy supper and discreet retirement behind a "Do Not Disturb" sign, she had to join him onstage during his concert. They were probably too happy and oblivious to notice any danger signs at the time. The couple didn't have time for a traditional honeymoon, but Julia occasionally joined Lyle on tour, uniting on stage where they sang an encore together. Months after their marriage, Lyle told an astonished reporter: "We've never spent more than seven days together in a row." They even maintained separate residences.

The couple didn't have time for a traditional honeymoon, but Julia occasionally joined Lyle on tour, uniting on stage where they sang an encore together.

Julia protested that the arrangement was working, telling the press that they were able to pretend they were a normal couple: "We get up in the morning, we have breakfast, he goes off to work, I go off to work, we come home at night, 'How was your day, dear?' The whole gig." But that didn't happen very often. There were other internal forces at work. Julia was becoming more cosmopolitan. She had purchased a New York penthouse where she hosted intimate, gourmet dinners at which guests read poetry aloud. Lyle still loved to get back to the farm where he tended the chickens and drove down dusty Texas back roads in his truck. His idea of a good meal was chicken or beef cooked up in the front yard fire pit.

The two did make a film together. Julia took a large cut in salary to appear in another Robert Altman multi-character drama, *Prêt-à-Porter* (called *Ready to Wear* in North America). It was Altman's take on the fashion industry and featured Sophia Loren, Marcello Mastroianni, Danny Aiello, Kim Basinger, Lauren Bacall, Linda Hunt and Rupert Everett, among others. Julia and Lyle didn't actually have a scene together, but it did put them, for a while, together in Paris. They were seen walking hand in hand along the Champs-Elysées.

Ready to Wear (1994)

Back home, Julia sometimes wore her wedding ring. Sometimes she didn't.

The *New York Post* broke the story (although the *National Enquirer* had long since suggested the relationship was deteriorating). The *Post* headline, on April 29, 1994, read, "Julia's Got a Hot Dinner Date & You Can Bet Lyle Won't Lovett."

The *Post* had photographed Julia and fast-rising movie heartthrob Ethan Hawke holding hands, dancing and embracing at Lola, a trendy New York hangout. Julia's quick damage control unit leaped into action saying that (ahem!) during those intimate wee hours of the morning, Julia and Ethan were discussing a movie they were planning to make together.

Meanwhile, Lyle had a few fires of his own banked in the barbecue. The ever-energetic *Enquirer* took photos of Lovett and a sexy blonde in a Texas motel. The blonde turned out to be an ambitious country singer named Kelly Willis. Ms. Willis and Mr. Lovett had apparently been involved for several months in a schizophrenic affair that was both public and private. On October 7, 1994, Lyle brought Kelly onstage during a concert at Austin's Paramount Theatre. He introduced her as his "favorite singer" and kissed her. They then sang one of Lyle's hits, "I Love Everybody."

But after the concert, while the tabloid press hung around the stage door hoping to get a glimpse (or a shot) of Julia, the James Bond stuff began. Lyle and Kelly left the theater at around 12:30 AM. Kelly drove off in the rain in her Toyota Tercel. Lyle left for the Four Seasons Hotel. All was quiet until about 4:00 AM, when Kelly sneaked out of her home and drove to the Four Seasons. She wasn't seen again until about 11:00 AM, in the

Meanwhile, Lyle had a few fires of his own banked in the barbecue. The ever-energetic ***Enquirer*** took photos of Lovett and a sexy blonde in a Texas motel.

lobby of the hotel. The two tried the same stunt the next night, but when they left the room together carrying their luggage, they were met by a photographer furiously snapping pictures. When she heard about it, Julia held her peace but was obviously distraught. She was so upset, in fact, that she was caught soon after sobbing on a New York park bench in the arms of (wait for it) Jason Patric.

Oprah Winfrey, who has been a friend, confidante and a public chronicler of Julia's life, managed to get through the spin and uncover the sad truth when Julia admitted to her in an interview that her marriage to Lovett was over. "I have understood since childhood that marriage was something you have to do," said Julia. "When Lyle came along I was pretty well swept away. It was like he put some voodoo spell on me."

> ***People*** **put the story on their cover, even relegating the Academy Awards, which were being staged at the same time, to an inside spread.**

After Julia wrapped the shoot and thankfully put *I Love Trouble* behind her, she had but a few days to appear on set in Beaufort, North Carolina, for her next project, *Grace Under Pressure.* Again, everyone had high hopes. The screenplay was written by Callie Khouri, who had just won an Oscar for her neo-feminist picture *Thelma & Louise.* Julia played Grace Bichon, who manages her father's (Robert Duval) riding stable. Grace is married to Eddy (Dennis Quaid), a roguish, happy-go-lucky sort who is engaged in an affair with a local woman. After Grace confronts Eddy in the middle of the night on the streets of their small town, she flees to her sister Emma Rae's (Kyra Sedgwick) to decide what to do about her uncertain future.

Julia liked her low-key but professional director, Lasse Hallström. The Swedish director had proven his ability to vividly capture small-town America in *What's Eating Gilbert Grape*, with Johnny Depp and Leonardo DiCaprio. Quaid, who had earlier overcome a debilitating drug habit, proved affable, and a solid relationship developed between the two stars personally

Something to Talk About (1995)

and on-camera. At the time, Quaid was happily married to Meg Ryan.

Despite the turmoil in her personal life, Julia felt happy shooting *Grace Under Pressure*, which was released in August 1995 under the title *Something to Talk About*. She found herself in a warm emotional bubble as she re-established her rapport with her surrogate family on the crew. Kyra Sedgwick recalled: "After the second day on the set, she knows everybody's name. She comes in every single morning, smiles and says, 'Hello so-and-so' to every member of the crew. She is constantly cracking jokes, even in the midst of a huge crying scene."

Something to Talk About didn't electrify the critics. Joe Baltake in the *Sacramento Bee* did observe: "Under Hallström's direction, *Something to Talk About* seems volatile and fresh as well as tender and sentimental." The film was a sincere effort and audiences responded by pushing its box office score to a respectable, if not spectacular, $50 million.

Julia's relationship with the press often depended on her mood, the state of her personal life or the pushiness of the journalist asking the questions. Generally, though, she regarded the press as her enemy. The more she tried to hide, the more the press pushed itself in her face. She hated living in the headlines but, like it or not, she was a tabloid magnet. And her chaotic relationships were the stuff of great copy.

Her feelings towards the millions of fans that supported her and bought tickets to her movies, were also ambivalent. Her fans continued to love her, but she desperately wanted her own space and kept them at a safe distance. One of the most common pictures

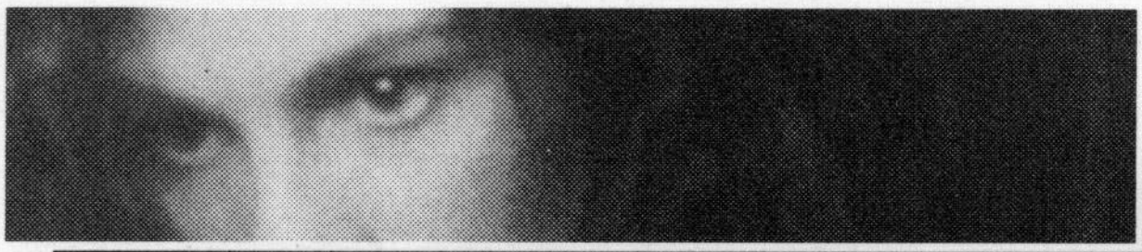

JULIA LOVE-LIFE UPDATE

In 1995, Julia hired a handsome, muscular personal trainer named Pasquale (Pat) Manocchia. He was a trainer for the stars and fitness consultant for *Good Morning America*. Manocchia remained Julia's number one guy throughout 1996.

taken of the star shows her striding past groups of admirers as they hold out pen and paper in hopes of an autograph. She ignores them with what has been termed her frozen "Stepford Wives" smile.

Julia's attitude towards press and public rose to its most irrational point when, in 1995, she accepted a six-day trip to Haiti as a Good Will Ambassador for UNICEF, a position that the late Audrey Hepburn had fulfilled with distinction and class. The idea was to focus public attention on the plight of Haiti's impoverished children. But Julia, completely missing the chance to make a positive influence, used the occasion to attack the photographers that followed her everywhere for what was in essence an elevated photo-op. In a hot, overcrowded classroom she felt that one photographer was too aggressive and yelled at him: "You in the orange shirt. Out!" Julia remembers it differently, but her actions soured the occasion. At an official cocktail party in her honor (well-attended by the press), she showed up in overalls. When the photographers arrived, the security guards made sure their lenses were covered and pushed them around.

The next photo-op was to be a barbecue the following day. The press found themselves disinvited. The UN Children's Fund formally apologized for the slight and suggested that Julia's behavior could be attributed to "shyness" and "inexperience in her new role." Julia, unabashed, rationalized her inexplicable behavior by saying that even negative publicity "brings attention to the plight of the poor children of Haiti."

In 1990, an American writer, Valerie Martin, fashioned her own take on Robert Louis Stevenson's creepy tale *The Strange Case of Dr. Jekyll and Mr. Hyde* and wrote the bestseller *Mary Reilly*. In her story, an unschooled maid becomes an unwilling witness to the horrific events that transpire in the Jekyll household. Christopher Hampton, who penned the Oscar-winning *Dangerous Liaisons*, wrote the screenplay for the film, and the directorial reins were handed over to the respected British filmmaker Steven Frears (*Dangerous Liaisons*, *Prick Up Your Ears*).

John Malkovich signed on to play Jekyll/Hyde, and Julia Roberts was considered for the role of the plain, mousy maid—an interesting piece of casting. Frears, however, was enchanted by the actress. Said one executive, picking up on Frears' obsession: "I remember she walked past me on the way to the set. You wanted to put your arms around her and say, 'It's going to be all right.' She just exudes vulnerability and a need for affection in this role." Tri-Star paid $10 million to the pretty woman and then dressed her down to look like dowdy servant. Julia played the role of Dr. Jekyll's timid maid swathed in a long-sleeved, high-necked servant's dress with a bonnet atop a scraggly wig. She bleached out her eyebrows. Her celebrity presence vanished, and she became a humble, rather unremarkable-looking waif.

As if rebelling against her larger-than-life image, Julia reveled in making herself as plain as possible. It took the makeup crew two hours each morning to turn the star into a nondescript Scottish domestic. On-camera, she appears meek and often terror-stricken, not really understanding the horrors going on in Dr. Jekyll's laboratory. Fellow cast members, many

As if rebelling against her larger-than-life image, Julia reveled in making herself as plain as possible.

of them with considerable experience on the English stage, were impressed with her dedication and professionalism.

Frears demanded many rewrites, and Hampton complied, observing later: "It was the sort of rewriting that destroys all rhythms. The script was expanded to half its length again, from 85 pages to 130. Then the film gets made, it's too long, it's cut down, and you lose all cohesion in the process."

The studio took one look at Frear's final cut of the film and took it away from him. They re-cut it and showed it to test audiences, who hated it so much that Tri-Star begged Frears to return and cut it again. The director agreed, but couldn't make it work any better the second time around.

The result was dreary and incoherent and pleased no one. Malkovich, for reasons known only to himself and perhaps to Frears, played Jekyll and Hyde as if they were pretty much alike. The climax, which was re-shot to elevate the horror, was neither horrible nor satisfactorily dramatic. Julia, who might have suggested seething but veiled Victorian passions, seemed flat and

Mary Reilly (1996)

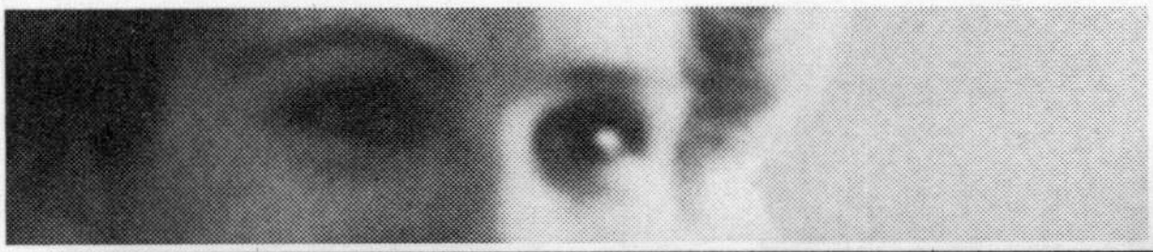

JULIA LOVE-LIFE UPDATE

In December 1995, Julia appeared in an episode of the highly rated sitcom *Friends*. Shortly after her appearance, she and one of the stars, Matthew Perry, dated. Julia declined to give their short time together any emotional weight beyond just a few dates. "We were friends," she told the ever-present press. "Went out on a bunch of dates, had fun, but the 'love affair' never existed. For that to happen, I think, people being in love with each other helps."

uninteresting. The young actress just didn't have the acting chops necessary to delve into the psychosexual depths that dripped from the gothic pages of the book. *The New York Times* observed sadly that Julia was "solemnly repetitive without much spark." There was no chemistry between Malkovich and Roberts, and the rest of the cast seemed more like wax figures than real people.

When it was released in February 1996, the $39 million project sank without leaving many ripples behind. Julia moved on to her next project, a biopic of the Irish firebrand, Michael Collins, which would reunite her with one-time lover Liam Neeson.

Wouldn't you have loved to have been a fly on the wall when Liam Neeson told his lovely new wife Natasha Richardson about his female love interest in his new film? Michael Collins was one of the founders of the Irish Republican Army. Neeson was the logical actor to play the part, and Julia Roberts would play the role of Collins' long-time companion Kitty Kiernan. Long nights in Ireland, working intimately with a woman who had a well-deserved reputation for sexual encounters with her co-stars? It must have been quite a conversation.

★★★

chapter 10

"Which One of You Gunslingers is Going to Ask Me to Dance?"

The whole thing was conducted with reserve and decorum. Julia requested that director Neil Jordan ask Liam and Natasha if they would object to her playing his screen lover. "I was sure Liam wouldn't be embarrassed by my being his leading lady because we've remained friends over the years. And it was all a long time ago. What also helped was the fact that Natasha and I are great friends. I think they are the perfect couple."

"I was sure Liam wouldn't be embarrassed by my being his leading lady because we've remained friends over the years. And it was all a long time ago."

The delighted Jordan noted: "(Liam and Julia's) love scenes were tender, warm and very sexy. It helped the film enormously that they had once been an intimate couple. They were playing lovers, and so they didn't have to go through that awkward stage that actors usually do of getting to know each other."

Michael Collins begins with Ireland's bloody Easter Rebellion of 1916 and ends with Collins' murder. Collins developed innovative guerilla methods of warfare, which wounded the occupying British army so badly that they withdrew, bringing Ireland a degree of freedom but leaving behind a tension that still exists today. Julia shone in her role as Kitty, nailing the authentic Irish brogue. She also sang a lovely version of the traditional Irish folksong *She Moves Through the Fair*. Unfortunately for the actress, when it came to editing the film, Jordan went for the conflict rather than the love story, and many of her best scenes ended up on the cutting room floor. Her role became an extended cameo. She did get to wear some great period dresses, though.

Released in August 1996, the film met with mixed reviews, most notably *Newsweek*'s, which singled out Julia's performance: "*Mary Reilly* and *Michael Collins* proved that Roberts was not meant to time travel." Few viewers seemed interested in the life of the Irish revolutionary, and the film died having earned a paltry $10 million at the box office.

The song she warbled so pleasantly in the film was part of what Julia called "her summer of song." She also sang in Woody Allen's *Everyone Says I Love You*, in which she played the role of Von, a woman who tells her psychiatrist what she is looking for in the perfect lover. Woody played Joe, who is smitten with Von. With help from Von's eavesdropping daughters, he finds the way to their mother's heart. Julia took the part because she wanted to work

Everyone Says I Love You (1996)

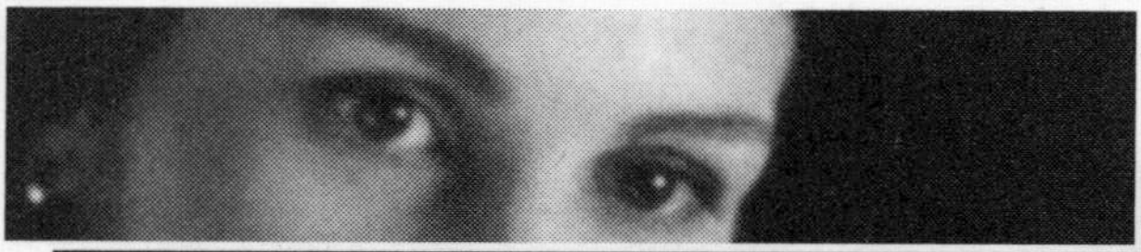

JULIA LOVE-LIFE UPDATE

On September 7, 1996, Julia went out on the town in New York with her latest beau, Pat Manocchia. The evening ended at the Hogs and Heifers Bar. The details are clouded in confusion, but at one point, Julia apparently removed her bra (a tradition in the club) while keeping her top intact. She later danced with and kissed, with some passion, a female waitress named Margaret Emery—another Hogs and Heifers tradition. Or so the story goes. At any rate, Julia's embattled press agent spent the next day fending off questions about whether Julia Roberts was a lesbian or not.

with Allen, who was known for writing Oscar-winning roles for women. Alas, there would be no Oscar for this film, and like most of Allen's latter-day efforts, it performed poorly at the box office.

Julia was now a major Hollywood star in serious decline and in desperate need of a hit.

It was time to get the Roberts ship back on course, and Julia did it with a no-brainer—an audience-friendly romantic comedy. *My Best Friend's Wedding* was a tonic for Julia and a blessed welcome for her ever-patient audience. She played Julianne Potter, a career-oriented food critic. In the film, Julianne makes a deal with her best friend Michael (Dermot Mulroney) that if, by the ripe old age of 28, neither has found their true love, they will marry each other. Michael does indeed find a candidate—a young thing named Kimmie (Cameron Diaz)—just as Julianne realizes that she has been in love with Michael all along. She flies to Chicago in an attempt to sink the upcoming nuptials.

My Best Friend's Wedding (1997)

Not only was Julia radiant in the film, but she turned in a robust comic performance. She performed a minor miracle and made the character quirky and endearing rather than the devious plotter she could have been. In keeping with her role as a 28-year-old diva, Julia also graciously gave away some great moments. Both Diaz and Rupert Everett, who played her editor and confidant, had show-stealing moments.

Not only did Julia establish a warm relationship with cast and crew, she was actually seen bantering with onlookers on exterior shoots in Chicago. When the film was released, both public and critics embraced it as a welcome return of the Julia they knew and loved. Said Ruth Stein in the *San Francisco Chronicle*: "Director P.J. Hogan knows how to show off his star, putting her in almost every scene. Roberts quickly establishes that she's worthy of the attention." Crowed *Newsweek*: "Julia Roberts is back in glorious comic form."

Audiences responded with "Pretty Woman where have you been?" *My Best Friend's Wedding* became the most successful romantic comedy *ever* at the box office when it was released in June 1997, recording $21 million on its opening weekend and moving towards a towering $126 million (domestic) and $165 million (worldwide). With the success of the film, Julia's asking price drifted upwards to a celestial $17 million.

About this time, Julia bought her dream home. She had already purchased a condo in the clouds—the penthouse of a Manhattan tower, where she staged her intimate salons. But there was still much of the southern belle about her, and perhaps she liked the down-home feel that Lyle Lovett's Texas farm had provided. At any rate, in September 1995, she bought a 50-acre adobe ranch near Taos, New Mexico, complete with indoor swimming pool, garages, a greenhouse, stock sheds, barn, corrals and a garden with a fountain. The price? $2.2 million. The 7000-square-foot,

"She's not very gracious when people go up to her or ask for an autograph. She just turns away when people approach her."

Territorial-style, four-bedroom, four-bath ranch also included seven horses and six dogs. It was a bit of a fixer-upper, but Julia fell to the task with enthusiasm. She was soon seen at the local Wal-Mart and supermarkets and bought thousands of dollars worth of local antiques. But her standoffish ways alienated many of the locals who thought she was a snob. She "rented" entire stores, kept everyone out and shopped by herself. One citizen grumped, "She's not very gracious when people go up to her or ask for an autograph. She just turns away when people approach her."

Julia enjoyed "fixing up" her little spread, and instead of hiring contractors, she did much of the work herself. Between shoots, she fired up her blue Ford tractor and tilled the dirt for her sunflower plantings. The actress/rancher stated that this pastoral retreat represented her "lessons learned." "I think that anybody who came here would say that this is a girl who understands and appreciates the quality of life," she said. In the distance, she could see New Mexico's majestic Sangre de Cristo Mountains.

> Coming off the hugely successful ***Lethal Weapon*** franchise, Warner Brothers was only too happy to press $80 million into the hands of producer Joel Silver, director Richard Donner and star Mel Gibson for their new project, ***Conspiracy Theory***, sight unseen. One quarter of the budget went to paying Gibson's salary.

The trio of filmmakers wanted Julia, but the Brothers Warner weren't too sure. Executives had heard about the problems largely attributed to Julia on the sets of *I Love Trouble* and *Hook*. Plus, Julia wanted $12 million. The studio believed that a lesser-known actress could carry the load, coasting on Gibson's box office clout. But Gibson was adamant, saying: "She is the queen of subtext. She's very expressive, very smart about the way she acts."

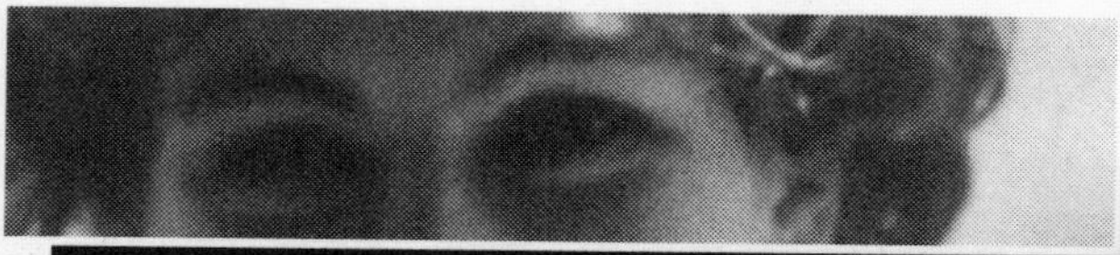

JULIA FAN FACT

Mel Gibson is a well-known goofball. Julia was attending a business meeting with her partner Elaine Goldsmith-Thomas in a suite at the posh Sherry-Netherland Hotel in New York when a door opened, revealing Gibson standing in the doorway with a lampshade on his head. "I was just trying not to be noticed," he said innocently.

Gibson prevailed, and Julia was hired to play Alice Sutton, a Justice Department agent who becomes the object of Jerry Fletcher's (Gibson) obsession after he rescues her from a mugging. Jerry is a New York cabby and something of a wacko—he combines everything he has heard into one grand, unified conspiracy theory. He tries to tell her of his fears, and she tries to humor him, until one day it appears that he may actually be correct.

The film had a quirky premise, but Donner smothered it with overproduction and bloated action sequences, causing Roger Ebert to comment: "Our eyes glaze over because we know the actors have gone out for lunch, and we are looking at stunt men supervised by the second unit."

Gibson (remember the lampshade?) is known for his practical jokes. On the first day of shooting, he sent Julia an expensive-looking present. When she

On the first day of shooting, he sent Julia an expensive-looking present. When she opened it, she found a freeze-dried rat.

opened it, she found a freeze-dried rat. Julia gave back as good as she got. She arrived at work one morning early, sneaked into Gibson's Winnebago and saran-wrapped his toilet bowl. When the actor relieved himself, the bowl overflowed, ruining an expensive pair of boots. "I was tap-dancing like Gene Kelly in *Singin' in the Rain*," he admitted ruefully.

Conspiracy Theory was a manufactured product of the Hollywood machine and not much of a movie. The reviews were almost universally bad, but the film coasted to a $137 million take at the box office on the strength of its two stars.

In November, Julia met the man who was to become one of the great romantic experiences of her life. His name was Benjamin Bratt. He was an academically trained actor who achieved his first great success from 1995 to 1999, as dapper Detective Reynaldo Curtis in the TV series *Law & Order*. Bratt is devilishly handsome. He's tall (six-foot-two), an obvious Latino with an olive complexion and chiseled features. He is also suave and

Conspiracy Theory (1997)

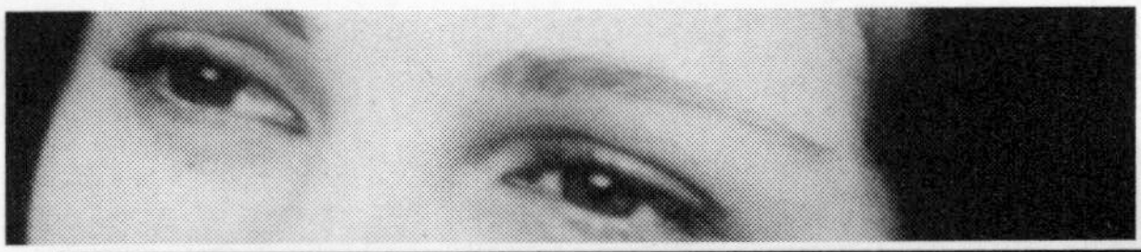

JULIA LOVE-LIFE UPDATE

For a while, Julia and a bartender named Ross Partridge were an item. She broke up with him in October 1997. The heartbroken Ross took to his bed and, said his mother, didn't get up for days.

exudes an Old World courtliness and enough electric charm to power much of Lower Manhattan. In 1999, *People* named him as one of the 50 most beautiful people of the year.

"It was like something hit me over the head with a bat," Julia said of her first glimpse of Bratt at an elegant French restaurant in Manhattan's SoHo district. Julia was still involved with Ross Partridge, but she was not one to allow the situation to pass without action. She sent the maitre d' over with a simple message: "Julia Roberts would like to buy you a drink."

Bratt was taken aback and somewhat skeptical. "It's a restaurant I frequent," he said, "and I thought one of my friends was playing a joke on me. I didn't want to impose on her, if that was the case, so I walked out without saying a word." The next day, Bratt began to worry that the message had been genuine, so he sent Julia, who by that time was on the West Coast, a note explaining the situation. Several months later, they had their first date.

"He is very good looking," said the smitten Julia, "and

> "I wondered if I was smart enough to know that it was the first kiss I'd ever had from the last person I'll ever choose to kiss every day."

all his handsomeness pales in comparison to his kindness. That is all a girl could ask for, really." Once their relationship had progressed to the first-kiss stage, Julia reported breathlessly: "I wondered if I was smart enough to know that it was the first kiss I'd ever had from the last person I'll ever choose to kiss every day."

After much tumultuous sailing on rocky emotional seas, Julia Roberts was about to dock in a quiet port with one of the most eligible bachelors in North America.

★★★

chapter 11

the world in a Frame

Julia could hear the creature's raspy breath in the jungle. He was standing about four feet behind her. Suddenly, a 400-pound male orangutan leaped forward. His long arms encircled her, crushing her to his chest. She was helpless. The camera crew attempted to pull her loose, but it was no use. They were grappling with a creature whose hands were the size of a human head and who possessed the strength of a man in just one of his fingers. Frightened, Julia just kept stroking the long, hairy arms. Then suddenly, the primate released her.

No, it wasn't Julia's worst nightmare. She had decided to take up a British production company's offer to go with them to the jungles of Borneo to host a documentary on the endangered primates. She'd leaped at the chance, actually. "I'd never been to that part of the world, and I love primates," said Julia. "I though it would be an adventure as well as doing something to raise awareness of the orangutans' terrible plight."

Julia came through her ordeal with Kusasi, the alpha male orangutan, with little trauma. "I firmly believe that he meant no harm to me. He was purely motivated by curiosity, wonderment and just wanted to be close to me for whatever reason—so I wasn't scared," she remembered later. For Julia, the three-week expedition, in the summer of 1997, was a dream. "We were a very small group, and we really had to pull together. Our trip, from start to finish, couldn't have been more hilarious, more enjoyable, more enchanting. Those guys are all English, and they are all very, very funny." The glamorous actress slept on a foam mattress thrown on a wooden floor. Many nights, she was afraid to sleep because of the spiders.

She enjoyed the experience so much that three years later, she traveled with a crew from the television series *Nature* to Mongolia. She spent two weeks with a nomadic family in their one-room transportable *ger*, their home. It had no bathroom, no running water and no heat. During that time, she got to know the family, milked a horse and even rode one of the wild ponies that form the basis of the nomads' society. At one point she helped the family members move their home. The men began to unwrap the *gers* in their camp and Julia pitched in. "It was like a party…I'm actually having a good time in the freezing cold, deconstructing a house. Who knew?"

For many years, after they met on the set of *The Player*, Susan Sarandon had been one of Julia's closest friends. "Have I gone to her house and boo-hooed about my pathetic life? Of course I have," Julia declares. "Did she fix it? She probably made me laugh."

Susan Sarandon first came to public attention as Janet, the innocent target of Dr. Frank 'N Furter in 1975's *The Rocky Horror Picture Show*. She has appeared, with distinction, in such films as

Stepmom (1998)

Bull Durham and *Atlantic City.* A consummate film actress, she has been nominated for an Academy Award four times, and finally won the accolade in 1996 as a sympathetic nun in *Dead Man Walking.*

Together, Sarandon and Julia shot the film *Stepmom,* which revolves around two children coping with their father's (Ed Harris) divorce and the new woman in his life. The "other woman," Isabel (Julia), is a successful photographer who does her best to treat the kids well, but does not intend to give up her career. Sarandon played Jackie, a full-time mother who regards Isabel as incompetent and fears for the emotional and physical well-being of her children. The conflict between them deepens when it is discovered that Jackie has cancer.

Julia also acted as executive producer of the film (Sarandon co-produced). It was Julia's first time in that position, and she took it very seriously, sitting in on script rewrites and production meetings with director Christopher Columbus. But when filming started, Julia says she left all that behind: "Once we started shooting, I was an actor. I mean, that's what I do. And that's enough. Particularly with this movie, I had enough on my plate."

Despite her years of friendship with Sarandon, Julia understandably felt a bit intimidated by her senior co-star. "I remember the first big rehearsal with Susan," she told a reporter during the press interviews just before the film was released. "Suddenly I thought, 'What if she thinks I suck?' That was the first time it occurred to me, 'Gee this could be bad.'" But Julia was on her best behavior, Sarandon is a professional and the atmosphere on the set was cordial but businesslike.

> "Once we started shooting, I was an actor. I mean, that's what I do. And that's enough. Particularly with this movie, I had enough on my plate."

Essentially a "chick flick," *Stepmom* was greeted with ambivalence by the critics when it was released in December 1998. "Roberts does an especially appealing job as the striving step-parent," said the *Los Angeles Times,* while the uber-hip *Village Voice*

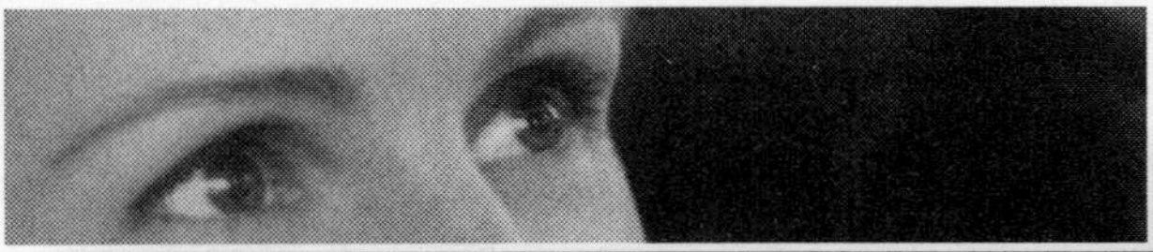

JULIA FAN FACT

Julia first met Hugh Grant when they both read for *Shakespeare in Love*. She loved Grant's performance in his star-making turn in *Four Weddings and a Funeral*.

trounced the film, only eking out a glimmer of praise for Julia: "Loathsome though *Stepmom* is, the eternally coltish Roberts is always a pleasure to watch." The film grossed an impressive $155 million worldwide.

The press might be excused for greeting Julia's proclamation of undying love for Benjamin Bratt with a degree of dubiousness. They had heard it many times before. *People* magazine's comment summed it up: "Roberts and long-term relationships are not the safest bets." Not wanting to repeat the failure she'd had with Lyle Lovett, Julia and Benjamin saw each other as often as possible and phoned daily. His *Law & Order* duties kept him in New York, and she was needed on sets in London and Maryland.

"You'd be surprised how normal our lives are together," said Bratt echoing statements made by other, earlier Roberts suitors. "We can walk around the streets of New York and San Francisco, and no one really bothers us. We just behave as we are—just human beings."

Marriage? Well, no, said Julia. Not yet. "Why is the media so impatient?" she demanded. "Its like 'Marry, have kids, get on with it!' Doesn't anybody understand that life just kind of flows?"

Bratt was effusive about his new partner. "We are together. Despite all the complexity and chaos that appear to exist in her life, she's also a very simple person. Simple in the most beautiful ways: generous, soulful, giving, humorous, loving—all those things that are important to me."

Writer Richard Curtis had written the script for *Notting Hill* with Julia in mind, and it came with English actor Hugh Grant attached. The story had Anna Scott, a Hollywood superstar, fall in love with a shy bookseller, William Thacker (Grant). Julia saw immediate parallels in her own life. She described Anna as being "still unsure about her own worth, whether as an actor or as a person. What is written about her concerns her a lot more than it would concern me. She's a lot more fragile."

Initially, though, Julia wasn't impressed. "How boring. How tedious," Julia told Curtis, producer Duncan Kenworthy and director Roger Mitchell over lunch in New York's Four Seasons Hotel. "Good luck with your film." But when she read the script, the actress fell in love with it. Chimed *Vanity Fair*: "Who better to play the world's most mythic, inaccessible and intimidating star than the world's most mythic, inaccessible and intimidating star."

Filming began in London's Notting Hill district in April 1998, and Grant, by his own admission, was as "skittish as a toad."

Notting Hill (1999)

JULIA LOVE-LIFE UPDATE

During the filming of *Notting Hill*, Julia and Benjamin flew by private jet to Naples and then sailed to Capri. The two conducted a private ceremony in which they exchanged gold wedding bands and pledged their love for one another, promising one day "to wed."

Julia was apprehensive about appearing with all these highly trained thespians (Grant was attending Oxford when she was still in high school in Smyrna, Georgia). She not only held her own in the film but developed a humorous, teasing familiarity with Grant. "Working with Hugh was fun," she laughed. "We had a great sense of fun, a lot of banter and an immediate rapport. From the first day of rehearsal, I just thought, 'We're going to get along quite easily'—and it was true." Grant found Julia "silly and teasable" and "couldn't have liked her more."

(The dashing Grant was less gallant on *The Oprah Winfrey Show* on October 26, 2004, when he observed that Julia was "very big mouthed. Literally, physically, she has a very big mouth. When I was kissing her, I was aware of a faint echo."

Oprah, ever the Julia pal, laughed but protested, "She's one of the nicest people I ever met."

"I wouldn't go that far," mused Grant.)

The world premiere of *Notting Hill*, on April 27, 1999, was a notable event. Grant squired his spectacularly beautiful then-girlfriend Elizabeth Hurley, whose appearances at premieres in very revealing outfits were legendary. Of course, the press was out in force looking to take pictures of the two so they could run comparisons the next morning. Julia wore a lovely red-sequined, knee-length dress designed by Vivienne Tam. But the kicker came when Julia raised her arm to wave to the assembled fans and revealed (horrors!) an unshaven armpit. The American reaction was muted, but the British tabloids broke into a major sweat. The headlines the next morning read "Do You Dare to Bare Your Hair?" and "Arms and the Woman."

> "From the reaction of the English press, you would have thought I had a chinchilla under there," protested Julia. "I thought I looked pretty. I had on a pretty dress, and I felt pretty."

No one remembers what Elizabeth Hurley wore to the London premiere.

Notting Hill opened in North America on May 28, 1999, and took in $22 million on its first weekend, breaking Julia's own box office record for *My Best Friend's Wedding*. For the New York premiere, Julia wore a full-length Calvin Klein dress with demure long sleeves and a high neckline.

So where, clamored the public and press, was the sequel to *Pretty Woman*? If the subtleties of the hooker and the millionaire had been exhausted in the first film, how about a film pairing the two stars, Richard Gere and Julia Roberts? Garry Marshall was looking for a suitable script and so was Gere. The actor found the story of a journalist who writes a satiric story about a woman who can't commit and jilts four men at the altar. Gere cast himself as Ike, the journalist, and he saw Julia as Maggie Carpenter, the subject of his column. In the film, Ike

> But the kicker came when Julia raised her arm to wave to the assembled fans and revealed (horrors!) an unshaven armpit.

travels to Maryland, where he learns about Maggie's goofy emotional fluctuations and aborted marriages. And, of course, he falls for her. Julia didn't like the script much. Neither did Sandra Bullock, Geena Davis, Ellen DeGeneres or Demi Moore, who all turned it down. Gere had it rewritten to beef up the woman's part, and Julia nibbled.

So, cast and crew and the two stars decamped for Maryland to shoot *Runaway Bride.* Once again the press was running a high fever. Here were two stars who may or may not have had an affair during their first film, now living together in the same bed and breakfast. Would Julia run true to form and abandon her current beau for her attractive co-star? The duo provided lots of fodder, with public demonstrations of mutual regard including a plethora of hugs and kisses. It seemed that history was about to repeat itself. But no, the bond with Bratt held true through it all. Julia talked to her lover on the phone every day. He even hung on when Gere gave her a big, wet kiss for her 31st birthday, while the cameras flashed. (Bratt was reportedly not impressed when he saw the pictures, but he persevered.)

Runaway Bride (1999)

As a film that was designed as a showcase for two twinkling stars, *Runaway Bride* also proved to be an audience pleaser when it was released in July 1999. The critics were less kind. Internet critic Moira MacDonald skewered: "It looks as if Julia and the horse were trying to get the hell away from the camera and into a better movie." But the audiences thumbed their noses at the critics. For the third time in a row, Julia broke her own record for a romantic comedy at the box office. Her price per film again drifted upwards to $20 million, putting her on a par with Tom Cruise and Tom Hanks—the only woman in Hollywood to dwell in those rarefied heights.

The one-time number one on Mr. Blackwell's Worst Dressed list had blossomed into a clotheshorse. Actually, Julia always dressed in reaction to the men in her life. With Kiefer and Jason Patric, she was the queen of castoffs, with a wardrobe that looked like it was on loan from the Salvation Army. She tended to dress "down home" while married to Lyle. But now she was the companion of a man who looked great in anything. Suddenly, Julia was appearing at intimate soirées and grand premieres in stunning clothes from the great fashion designers of our time.

"I'm a late-blooming clothes fanatic," she allowed. "Most girls go though this at 16 or 18. I've never had to get dressed for work. I could show up for shoots in pajamas and no one would care…I'm beginning to realize you can be comfortable, stylish and—dare I say—pull off the whole sexy thing…I'm in a phase where style is becoming a fun issue, a sporting event."

"I'm a late-blooming clothes fanatic," she allowed. "Most girls go though this at 16 or 18. I've never had to get dressed for work. I could show up for shoots in pajamas and no one would care…"

She appeared in fashion shoots for *Harper's Bazaar* and *In Style*. The *In Style* spread was the most spectacular. The magazine sent her to Venice with a stunning wardrobe of styles from Malo, Vera Wang, Dolce & Gabbana, Feretti and Valentino. Now in her thirties, Julia was growing up. The one time "coltish" and awkward, badly dressed starlet had developed a strong and seemingly long-term relationship, was back on top of the heap in the most cut-throat business in the world and had evolved into a dazzling clotheshorse with exquisite taste.

Erin Brockovich, in person, is an eyeful. She stands 5 feel 10 inches tall, wears a 34DD bra and totters about on high heels. In 1981, she was voted Miss Pacific Coast and enjoyed the beauty queen circuit so much that she quit her job and went at it full time. Along the way she had three children and divorced two husbands, then tired of it all and joined a law office. She had no money, no resources and little education, but through obsession and hard work, she put together a case against the mighty Pacific Gas and Electric Company over the harm its toxic waste had caused the citizens of Hinkley, California. She ultimately helped win the largest settlement in a direct-action lawsuit in U.S. history—$333 million. Brokovich struggled through it all, often going without food herself so her kids could eat.

What a woman. What a story. Julia read the script Susannah Grant had written for Danny DiVito's Jersey Films and immediately expressed interest to the producers. Cult director (*sex, lies & videotape*) turned mainstream filmmaker (*Traffic*) Steven Soderbergh read it and quickly proclaimed, "I'm in." Producer Michael Shamberg phoned Julia in New York at the restaurant where his people were trying to persuade her to commit to the film. But he could only reach the waitress, who said, "Honey, the guy you're looking for wasn't here very long. Everybody's left already, and they sure didn't look very happy." Shamberg was crushed…until he heard Julia's highly recognizable guffaw. He had been talking with her all along, while she was doing her best cocktail waitress impression. "When do we begin?" she asked when she stopped laughing.

The long road to Oscar was about to begin.

★★★

chapter 12

"They're Called Boobs, Ed"

Erin Brockovich began filming in several small towns in California's Mojave Desert in May 1999. The budget was $55 million. Julia Roberts' salary accounted for a little less than half of that.

The transformation of Julia's 34B cup into the bounteous Brockovich bosom was a challenge for Hollywood makeover artists. Even Benjamin Bratt chimed in: "It takes a village to raise that cleavage." Several alternatives were considered, including prosthetic enhancements, but in the long run, Julia's own modest endowments pulled it off. "It doesn't involve pumps or levers or anything, just a little good old-fashioned know-how," was her comment. Upon release of the film, many viewers and reviewers noted Julia's successfully enhanced superstructure, although Roger Ebert suggested that her revealing costumes took away from plot development, placing "her character somewhere between a caricature and a distraction."

"I was fine in the shoes until I got everything else going, and there was the whole balance issue, because I was high and I was out far."

Julia hates high-heeled shoes. Wearing them "took a little practice," she joked good-humoredly. "I was fine in the shoes until I got everything else going, and there was the whole balance issue, because I was high and I was out far." The actress was also uncomfortable in the skirts and blouses that exposed more of her than she was used to. "I have something in my closet that I call a dress," she sighed. "There's something in her closet where the whole part that covers your ass just isn't there." But the star persevered. "I would come to work looking like a 14-year-old boy and get ready and then come back 45 minutes later, and people would be, like, 'What happened to you?'"

Julia's approach to the role was validated by her co-star, the veteran English actor and four-time Oscar nominee Albert Finney, who played Erin's boss, Ed Masry. Masry initially disliked the pushy Brockovich, but came to appreciate her drive and intelligence.

"Julia's commitment to this part really touched me," said the sometimes-irascible performer. "Working with her was enjoyable because it was volatile and unpredictable. I was proud of her as a fellow professional. That's how a trooper should be." The admiration was mutual. "I could not have achieved what I've achieved in this movie without him by my side, without his friendship and support. He's a man I really respect and love," said Julia.

Julia also learned to love and respect Steven Soderbergh—so much so that she would place herself in his hands again and again in the next few years. She referred to him as "a genius."

Erin Brockovich (2000)

Soderbergh was equally impressed. "I feel very lucky—like I was catching her at a real high point. It's like watching Michael Jordan drive the lane. She is at her absolute peak as an artist. Technically, she can do anything. She's one of the few actresses you can compare to Audrey Hepburn without being struck by lightning."

Hollywood felt the buzz, and for once the predictors were right. When *Erin Brockovich* was released on March 17, 2000, it became an instant smash. The film rang up $28.1 million in its opening weekend and went on to earn $125 million in the North American market and $132 million in the rest of the world. It also changed the industry's attitude towards Julia. She had previously been known as a lightweight performer with tremendous clout at the box office. But while *Erin Brockovich* still benefited from her "star quality" and good looks, it showed that she had matured as an actress—that she could "open" a dramatic film as well. Internet reviewer James Berardinelli rhapsodized: "With a performance that shows off both her comic and dramatic aptitude, Roberts brings the title character to life with a zest and intensity that may surprise viewers who have pigeonholed her into the *Runaway Bride* mold. This is not the first time Roberts has shown that she has unexpected range, but it may be the first time many people will recognize it." Jay Carr of the *Boston Globe* joined the chorus of convinced critics: "From start to finish, Roberts' warmth and energy pour off the screen in this film, which is boldly contoured to accommodate her outsized personality. Tapping into her high-strung maverick side, Roberts really makes this film stand up and march, or rather totter fearlessly ahead on eight-inch heels."

> "Technically, she can do anything. She's one of the few actresses you can compare to Audrey Hepburn without being struck by lightning."

Someone thought to ask Eric Roberts about his sister's triumph. His reply was hardly one to back up his claim that he wanted to patch things up with his her. The disgruntled actor noted: "I saw *Brockovich*, and I must say I wasn't that impressed. Everyone's going on about how great she was in it, but what did she do? Wear some push-up bras. It wasn't great acting."

The Academy of Motion Picture Arts and Sciences begged to differ. When the nominations came in, to no one's surprise (except possibly Eric's), Julia received a Best Actress nomination. The film was also nominated for Best Picture and Best Supporting Actor (Albert Finney), and earned nods for Best Screenplay and Best Director (Soderbergh).

Julia and Benjamin Bratt arrived at the Shrine Auditorium on March 25, 2001, not in the traditional limousine, but in a black Ford Expedition sport utility vehicle. Julia wore a 1982 vintage black Valentino dress with white piping. She also sported a diamond bracelet worth over $1 million, loaned to her by Van Cleef & Arpels. She looked lovely.

> **To no one's surprise (she had won just about every other major award for her performance), when Kevin Spacey tore open the envelope on the stage of the Shrine Auditorium, the winner was..."Julia Roberts for *Erin Brockovich*."**

Julia wobbled her way to the stage. She was not used to wearing high heels, so Bratt gallantly assisted her. When she finally navigated onto the stage she hugged Spacey and cried out, "I'm happy!" More than a little flustered and knowing she was going to run out of time, she looked down on conductor Bill Conti in the pit and spiritedly demanded: "And, sir, you're doing a great job. But you're so quick with that stick, so why don't you sit because I may never be here again." The audience burst into applause. The flustered star paid tribute to the other nominees and thanked Albert Finney. Then she singled out Steven Soderbergh: "You made me want to be the best actor that I suppose that I never knew I could be, or aspire to and I made every attempt—Stick Man, I see you (she said again to Conti). So thank you for really making me feel so...I love it up here." Julia thanked her family and her boyfriend, and finished off with: "I love the world. I'm so happy. Thank you."

Later she apologized for forgetting to acknowledge the founder of her feast—Erin Brockovich. In an interview after the show, she voiced her feelings: "During my out-of-body experience earlier tonight, I didn't acknowledge her, shamefully, shamefully. And, really, she is the center of the universe which was our movie. And, I've said too many things and so many things to her that she knows the esteem in which I hold her, which is quite, quite high. But I was remiss in not acknowledging her tonight. So, with great humility, I acknowledge her profusely."

That evening, Benjamin Bratt wore an Armani tuxedo that matched Julia's dress. They also wore the rings that made people wonder if the couple would be tying the knot soon. But it was all a show. They had actually split up weeks before the Oscars but, in order not to wreck Julia's chances of winning, they kept quiet.

The couple gave no reasons for the breakup, but the media-fueled rumor mill was pleased to present the public with a smorgasbord to choose from. They were too busy to maintain a relationship. Julia was the big star making lots of money—Benjamin was not. George Clooney, Julia's co-star in *Confessions of a Dangerous Mind*, was blamed. George declined the honor, and said with a twinkle: "I didn't have time. I was too busy breaking up Tom and Nicole."

The world heard the official news about the breakup on, of all places, *The David Letterman Show*. Letterman's bandleader Paul Shaffer rudely asked Julia on the air, "So Julia, are you getting laid these days?"

"Bad, bad Paul," she scolded. "This is so wrong. I didn't come out of a cake. I'm shocked."

Letterman tut-tutted at Paul, but asked, "But what about it?"

"I love Benjamin. He's a good man, he's a fine man. He is, to the exultation of the single female population, not my man any more. Sad but true."

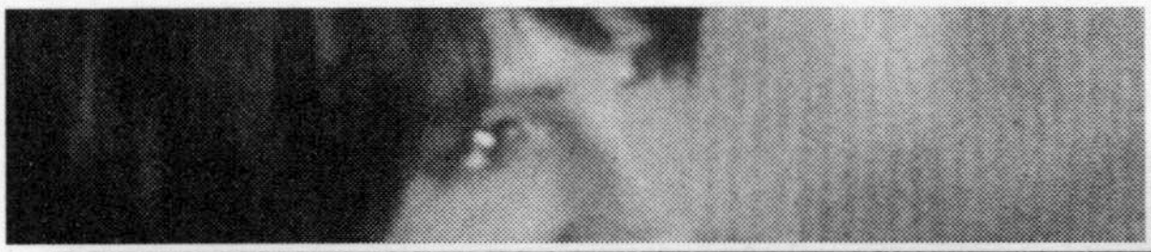

JULIA FAN FACT

All together, Julia's movies have grossed more than those of any other actress in Hollywood history—over $1 billion.

So Julia followed the lead and replied, "[The relationship]...has come to a kind and tenderhearted end, and my only regret is that, in some odd form though, the media, not surprisingly, cannot accept that it's tender hearted and kind. It had to be messy and ugly. Here's the thing. I love Benjamin. He's a good man, he's a fine man. He is, to the exultation of the single female population, not my man any more. Sad but true. We were just two kids trying to find our way in the world." And then she turned to Paul and said, "And to go back to your question, Paul, the answer is no."

After the heady success of *Erin Brockovich*, Julia tripped and fell with the movie *The Mexican*. It paired her with another box office god, Brad Pitt, and turned out to be anther inflated studio release that spent more on the salaries of its stars than on making a real motion picture. The main problem was that it featured two separate but intertwined stories. Pitt and Roberts had only about 20 minutes of onscreen time together and, as one reviewer pointed out, they played little more than cameos in each other's movies. Pitt played likeable goofball Jerry Welbach, an inept young mob messenger trying to get out. He is told to take one last assignment: go to Mexico and bring back a beautifully made pistol (called the "Mexican"). The second plot involves Jerry's girlfriend, Samantha Barzel (Roberts), who is furious that Jerry has taken another job with the mob. She decides to drive to Las Vegas alone and is kidnapped by another hit man (*The Sopranos*' James Gandolfini), who turns out to be sensitive and gay. He and Sam develop a friendship on the road. Meanwhile, Jerry has great problems with the "Mexican," which gets stolen several times.

Jerry knows that if he can't get it back to the mob, he will be rubbed out himself. The project was originally designed to be a small, quirky production with a $10 million budget, but it grew out of proportion as more money and bigger stars got thrown into it, and the budget ballooned to $35 million.

As was her wont, Julia bonded with the crew on *The Mexican.* And there was this cameraman named Dan Moder... He was young—33 years old—and boyishly handsome. Julia was sitting with Pitt, the story goes, when she looked up over her dark glasses and saw the burnished, muscular cameraman stripped to the waist and glistening with sweat. She asked Pitt, "Who's that young hunk a' burnin' love?"

Pitt puckishly reproved her, "Now, you be a good girl, or I'm gonna tell on you."

"Honey," Julia replied, "someone needs to strip that boy down, wash him up good and bring him to my trailer." She then got up and went over to talk to Moder. Tales from the set suggest that Julia began sending Moder "suggestive" messages. What Julia

The Mexican (2001)

didn't know (although it probably wouldn't have bothered her much) was that the cameraman was married. When she found out, Moder told Julia that his relationship with his wife, a pretty Argentinean makeup artist named Vera Steinberg, was just about over. With the two in close proximity on the set every day, the whispered conversations and mash notes quickly morphed into a flaming affair.

And all this happened a year before Julia and Benjamin officially broke up.

The Mexican enjoyed a robust opening in March 2001 thanks to its headliners, then quickly tanked. It finally made about half the take-home of *Erin Brockovich*. The marketing of the picture didn't help. It's not the first time Hollywood sold the sizzle rather than the steak, but the ads promised two beautiful stars in a slam-bang romantic adventure. "Brad and Julia Together" and "Love With The Safety Off" headlines trumpeted over photos of the two almost kissing. Peter Travers of *Rolling Stone* called it "a dream casting coup that promises a road movie of blissful comic romance (and) delivers a series of dramatic dead ends."

The solicitous makeup artist offered to adjust the chair to allow Julia to sleep.

"Why would I want to sleep and wake up 60 pounds heavier? I may never sleep again," protested the star.

The 60 pounds were the result of heavy makeup and a fat suit, necessary for Julia's character in her new film *America's Sweethearts*. Julia hated it—not only the sight of her overweight self but the long makeup sessions. "Not to be indiscreet," she lamented, "but the boobs were so heavy. All day my

"Why would I want to sleep and wake up 60 pounds heavier? I may never sleep again," protested the star.

back hurt. And I'm like, 'God, why do I feel like I'm put together wrong?'"

America's Sweethearts tells the story of Gwen (Catherine Zeta-Jones) and Eddie (John Cusack), married movie stars on the way to an acrimonious divorce, who pretend their marriage is still happy for the sake of their new film (further echoes of Julia's life?). Julia played Kiki, Gwen's mousy sister and assistant, who is overweight (hence the fat suit) but slims down and secretly falls in love with Eddie. Julia took the role when her old friend producer/director Joe Roth asked her to participate. Others in the film include Robert Downey Jr. (later replaced by Hank Azaria when Downey Jr. was arrested on drug charges) as Gwen's Latino boyfriend, as well as Stanley Tucci and Christopher Walken.

The script, written by Billy Crystal and Peter Tolan and picked up by long-time producer and studio head Joe Roth, spoofed the dreaded Hollywood tradition of the press junket. Junkets, generally held on weekends, involve entertainment journalists from all over the world gathering to meet the stars of a new release.

America's Sweethearts (2001)

The junketeers get to live like movie stars for a few days and spend a few minutes interviewing the stars before a television camera. The stars partake in press junkets because it's expected of them or because they have a particular interest in promoting the film, but they always find the interviews long and tedious, with the same questions being asked over and over in overheated hotel rooms.

The junkets tend to feel surreal—the real world recedes, and everyone gets caught up in the hype and says what they are expected to say whether it's the truth or not. It's this otherworldly element that Billy Crystal zeroed in on in his often-hilarious screenplay. The writers and producers decided to group all of *America's Sweethearts'* box office titans at a resort in the American Midwestern desert to enact the press junket. Many real junketeers were rounded up to appear in the film, and several them had on-camera speaking roles.

Sony, the producing company, decided on a daring ploy. They would release the film as counter-programming on July 20, 2001, opposite the guaranteed box office blockbuster *Jurassic Park III.* "We think there's a great advantage to having a Julia Roberts comedy in that slot. Midsummer is always a great opportunity for a romantic comedy with big movie stars," a studio executive stated.

The junketeers, who often tend to be enthusiastic about films that have wined and dined them, generally loved the movie. (If you see the quote "funniest movie of the year" or "white-knuckle, roller-coaster ride" in movie ads, you are probably reading the words of someone who attended a junket.) Other reviewers weren't quite so enthusiastic. The magisterial *New York Times* thundered: "Like a bottle of lukewarm champagne—an expensive one judging

The junkets tend to feel surreal—the real world recedes, and everyone gets caught up in the hype and says what they are expected to say whether it's the truth or not.

by the label—*American's Sweethearts* opens with a burst of effervescence and quickly goes flat." The public, however, liked what they saw and sent the project steaming to a $93 million take in North America and another $157 worldwide.

In big, black headlines, the *National Enquirer* blared: "Julia Roberts Runs Off With Married Man." An inquiring reporter tracked down Vera Steinberg, Moder's wife, to have her "tearfully" comment on the phone: "I don't have the whole story. Julia has the whole story. Why don't you call Julia and ask her what she did?" Vera had known something was up when she came across a phone bill with a great number of calls to Julia.

When she confronted her husband, he (reportedly) protested: "What do you think, I'm having some kind of affair with Julia Roberts? What would Julia Roberts want with me?"

When Vera finally uncovered the truth, Danny Moder had already moved out of his Woodland Hills, California, home. Reportedly, Danny's sister confronted Julia with: "What exactly do you want from my brother? Don't you realize that he's married?"

"Yes, I do," said Julia. "But Danny swore to me that he and his wife are through. I love Danny, and I believe he loves me."

Before long, the two had moved into a luxurious apartment on

"I don't have the whole story. Julia has the whole story. Why don't you call Julia and ask her what she did?"

Sunset Boulevard in Brentwood. They kept a low profile—many of the building's tenants didn't know Danny and Julia were there until months after they'd moved in. The other residents were not very happy when the tabloids discovered what they dubbed "the love nest" because hordes of reporters began camping outside, waiting for a glimpse of the fugitive lovebirds. On several occasions, police were called. Julia, who had become very adept at dodging the media, did the laundry and the shopping herself. The tabloid bloodhounds leaped on every scrap of information, and if there wasn't any, they made it up. When Danny's mother died of a heart attack on August 21, 2001, the family blamed Julia. Julia offered to pay for the funeral but that backfired. "Friends" were quoted to say: "The Moders are fuming over Julia's brash attempts to crash their mother's memorial."

And just when it seemed that things couldn't get worse, they did. Julia made a series of professional moves that again threatened her career.

★★★

chapter 13

life at the Top

Ocean's Eleven wasn't a film that cried out to be remade. The original had been a minor hit for Frank Sinatra and his Rat Pack (Dean Martin, Joey Bishop, Peter Lawford and Sammy Davis Jr.) back in 1960. But Steven Soderbergh, perhaps spurred by his artistic and box office success with *Eric Brockovich* and *Traffic*, felt that he could make a glossy, star-laden vehicle out of the '60s heist film and have a good time doing it.

To play Danny Ocean, everyone's favorite scoundrel and the leader of band of merry thieves, he turned to his partner in the Section 8 film production company, George Clooney. The two then contacted Brad Pitt, Matt Damon, Don Cheadle, Carl Reiner and Elliot Gould to play members of the gang. The $20 million fee apiece for Clooney, Pitt and Damon alone would have put the budget into the stratosphere, so the duo persuaded the mega-stars to go for "back-end participation," or a cut of the profits. They settled on 5 percent of the box office profits, and since the film made $183 million in North America alone, it proved to be a shrewd financial move.

Julia asked Soderbergh if there was a part for her, and the director said no, assuming that the cameo role of Danny's wife, Tess Ocean, was too small for a star of her stature. He sent Julia the script anyway, and she loved it. She liked the idea of the sophisticated settings, tight heist-movie scripting and playing dress-up. "You won't believe the costumes," she glowed in an interview. "I'm all glammed out—covered in Tiffany diamonds, from head to toe, with all this upswept hair and really fancy dresses." Besides, she adored Soderbergh and wanted to work with him again, and the whole experience looked like a fun way to spend a few weeks.

The script cut away the original film's six-casino heist, reducing it to three. The new plot now mostly revolved around Danny's jealousy over icy casino owner Terry Benedict's (Andy Garcia) relationship with his ex-wife (Julia).

The original Rat Pack took over Las Vegas in a bacchanalian revel that included gambling, "booze and broads" and appearances on each other's shows on the Strip. Now, the modern media was salivating in the hope that this new incarnation would perform in the same manner. But much to their disappointment, although the stars had a lot of fun, it occurred mostly behind closed doors, and Soderbergh's professional work ethic prevailed.

The film was released with predictable results just after Christmas 2001. The critics generally loved it, calling the film "a diverting romp," but also noting that it wasn't a good idea to examine the mechanics of its convoluted plot too closely—they didn't make a lot of sense. Clooney and Pitt had a good-natured screen relationship that generated more chemistry than the Monsanto corporation. Strangely, despite the close relationship of Soderbergh and Roberts, Julia didn't come off all that well. Her small

Ocean's Eleven (2001)

and thankless role was more a plot device than anything else. As the ex-wife who wants nothing to do with Danny Ocean, she frowned a lot and looked uncomfortable, despite her fancy gowns and jewels. And surprisingly, the director didn't help her much—with his lighting and camera angles, he made the star look tense and unappealing for much of the 15-odd minutes that she appears onscreen.

In 2002, Julia agreed to appear in Soderbergh's low-budget, all-digital experimental feature *Full Frontal.* The film tells the story of seven Hollywood types on various rungs of the success ladder whose lives intertwine. Julia's co-stars included David Duchovny (*The X-Files*) and David Hyde Price (TV's *Frasier*). Soderbergh was determined to keep the film small in every sense. His rules of conduct became the talk of Hollywood. His stars were paid scale—for Julia that was $25,000. She had to drive herself to the set. He demanded that his performers feed themselves at home before they arrived on set, be prepared to be photographed at any time, which included getting out of their cars on the way to work, and provide their own wardrobe and makeup. Some critics found

Full Frontal (2002)

the result mildly interesting, while others termed it confusing, self-indulgent and pointless. Said David Elliott in the *San Diego Union-Tribune*: "So much facile technique, such cute ideas, so little movie." No one expected the film to make much money. And it didn't. It barely returned its initial budget of $2 million.

Julia's next film also featured her in a cameo role. George Clooney was making his directorial debut in a quirky exercise called *Confessions of a Dangerous Mind: An Unauthorized Biography*. Clooney was set appear in it also, since his box office clout was the only way the loopy film could get made. (Clooney also threw in Matt Damon, Brad Pitt and Drew Barrymore in very small roles.) The film purported to be the story of Chuck Barris' double life. Barris was the creator of TV's *Dating Game* and host of the wacky *Gong Show*. In his autobiography, Barris maintained that at the same time he was a game show host, he was also a secret hit man for the FBI. Clooney made no claims about the veracity of the story. He simply filmed the Barris biography with all the outrageous (and unproven) claims the man had made.

Julia had the small role of an FBI operative. Some critics felt that the stunt casting didn't work. The *New York Times* noted: "When Julia Roberts shows up as a slinky double agent in hats that Diana Vreeland might have chosen, *Confessions* slides dangerously close to *Rocky and Bullwinkle*." Generally, though, the reviews were positive. Peter Travers stated in *Rolling Stone*: "*Confessions* isn't always coherent, but it's sharply comic and surprisingly touching, so hold the gong."

The film was released twice by the producing company Miramax in hopes that it would find an audience. Perhaps it was just too far out for mainstream filmgoers, but *Confessions of a Dangerous Mind* was finally deemed a noble failure.

In his autobiography, Barris maintained that at the same time he was a game show host, he was also a secret hit man for the FBI.

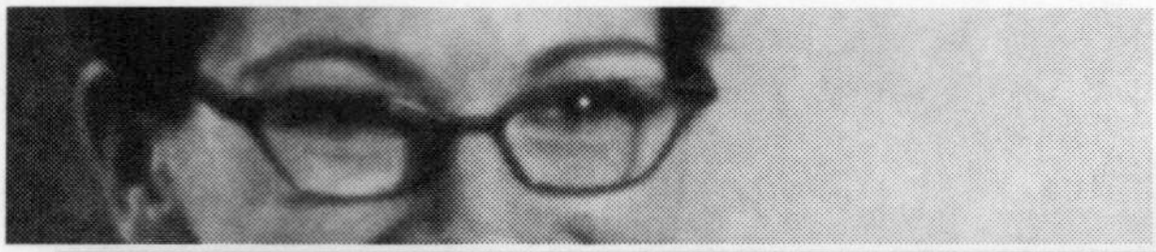

JULIA FAN FACT

In 2001, Julia played a small role alongside Bruce Willis in a rodeo film called *Grand Champion* for her friend, director Barry Tubb. She also helped finance the indie movie.

The idea of a major star making small, independent films is not a bad one. Well-received movies like *sex, lies & videotape* or *Sideways* can make an actor's career. They can also provide an actor with new challenges and a chance to escape the big-budget blues that often arise when the performer plays a supporting role to computer generated effects, explosions, car chases and alien attacks. And when an actor gets overexposed in a certain kind of film, independent movies can provide an outlet that keeps him or her working in the public eye, but perceived in a different light. When Bruce Willis found himself typecast as an action star, he found a lean-budgeted, tightly scripted indie he liked and played a small but pivotal role in Quentin Tarantino's *Pulp Fiction*. The film went on to become the most successful independent movie ever made, and Willis found his career rejuvenated.

After *Confessions* and *Full Frontal*, there was much questioning of Julia's choices and suggestions that her career was in decline. In 2002, Julia's one-time co-star, Cameron Diaz, claimed the crown as Hollywood's best-paid female star. That same year, however, *Forbes* named Julia number 26 on its annual list of the 40 richest people in America under 40 years of age. The magazine estimated her worth at $145 million.

Julia was, once again, trying to keep her emotional life from engulfing her. Her fans seemed willing to wait and keep the faith, as if they somehow knew that another film was in the works, one that would confound the naysayers and push her back to her accustomed place at the summit of the Hollywood hill.

Vera Steinberg made it clear to the press that she was in no hurry to forfeit her husband to Julia Roberts. She told anyone who would listen: "Julia Roberts stole my husband."

"He's obsessed," she said. "He really believes he's going to succeed where all those famous actors failed to get Julia down the aisle. I warned him, 'She'll chew you up and spit you out,' but he wouldn't listen. She's a mega-star and I'm a nobody—but I loved and cherished Danny and wanted to spend the rest of my life with him."

That firestorm was having an effect on Julia as well. Her previous escapades were blamed on hormones and a devil-may-care lifestyle. Now, for the first time, she was being branded a "scarlet woman" for breaking up a marriage. Her name was linked to that of Liz Taylor, a headline-grabbing marriage-buster of a previous generation.

Not all the Moder family hated her, though. Julia spent time with Danny's father, Mike, at his lakeside vacation home in the San Bernardino Mountains. Danny and Julia enjoyed an relaxing weekend at his dad's rustic place. Julia apparently enraptured the elder Moder in the same way she had charmed the son, and just before they left, he gave them his blessing.

Vera decided to contest Danny's divorce and reportedly accused Julia of "turning Danny's head with sex and throwing in offers of work in upcoming movies as a bonus." Julia decided to begin a campaign of her own. She appeared in a very public place with a white t-shirt that read "A Low Vera." Julia was chided for immaturity and lowering the level of the conflict. One Hollywood divorce lawyer was quoted as saying: "Here she is, one of the most powerful women in Hollywood, beating up on a jilted wife." Even Mike Moder rumbled his disapproval of the tacky gesture. Vera didn't help, however, when she replied with a t-shirt that read "Pretty Ugly Woman."

Now, for the first time, she was being branded a "scarlet woman" for breaking up a marriage. Her name was linked to that of Liz Taylor, a headline-grabbing marriage-buster of a previous generation.

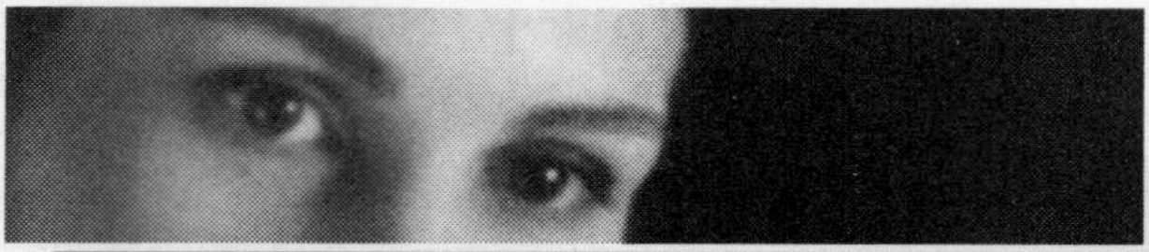

JULIA LOVE-LIFE UPDATE

Julia enjoyed making *Ocean's Eleven* with George Clooney. They indulged in a bit of dirty dancing at a party shortly after the film commenced, and there were reports of some "smooching" on the set. But then, Julia "smooched" most of her co-stars. George paid $1000 for a hug and kiss from Julia at a crew auction.

Apparently, when Vera threatened to hold up the divorce for another two years, Julia offered to buy her out—$200,000 to move the suit along. Vera declined, hoping, she said, that she and Danny would reconcile. When Danny told her there was no hope and Julia upped the offer to $400,000, Vera gave in. The divorce became final on May 6, 2002. Julia and Danny threw a celebration party in Cabo San Lucas, Mexico. No one from the Moder family showed up.

On July 2, Julia threw an Independence Day celebration at her ranch in New Mexico. Again, the Moder family declined to join them until Danny told them, in secret, that the party was a ruse. Guests arrived from all over the continent for the event. Members of Julia's family (except for her brother, who was not invited) filtered in. Bruce Willis showed up, as did Steven Soderbergh. Brad Pitt and Jennifer Aniston sent their regrets, as did George Clooney, who was in Kentucky attending the funeral of his aunt, Rosemary Clooney.

Shortly before midnight, Danny and Julia disappeared, then reappeared minutes later in more formal clothes. The desert stars glittered overhead and a gentle breeze blew from the Sangre de Cristo Mountains as the couple said their wedding vows. The two stood under a canvas roof in a circle of flower petals. He wore tan pants and a deep red shirt with ruffles down the front and on the cuffs. Julia's outfit, a creation from Los Angeles designer Judith Beylerian, featured a faded pink halter-top and an empire-waist dress accented with pearls, antique beads and handpainted flowers. In her upswept hair, the bride wore a small flower tiara. Not barefoot this time, she wore flat-heeled shoes. The ceremony took 20 minutes and when it was over, a Navajo shaman gave the couple his blessing. After the wedding, the guests danced to country music, as well as Elvis, Sting and Fatboy Slim, until dawn. When the weekend celebration ended, Julia and Danny drove to Los Angeles, where they fulfilled some business commitments before pointing Julia's Toyota Land Cruiser towards the San Ysidro Mountains and a two-day honeymoon. Julia's effusive description of her new husband shortly after the wedding had a familiar ring: "Danny is astounding. He's formidable. He's a man among men, unselfish and all encompassing, and he stands by the choices that he's made. He'll never blame it on somebody else."

Vera Steinberg continued to be unimpressed. She predicted the marriage wouldn't last a year. "Danny cheated on me, and he'll cheat on her," she said. The media went into full attack mode and published many reports of an imminent breakup. There were stories of public rows and of Julia stalking out of parties. But Julia and Danny, apparently very happy, celebrated their first anniversary during a romantic idyll in a medieval castle in Italy.

The film *Mona Lisa Smile* takes place on the campus of the staid New England Wellesley College during the 1953–54 academic year. Julia played Katherine Watson, a new art history teacher. At first, Katherine is excited about the prospect of interacting with a student body comprised of the most intelligent women in the United States. But what she finds disappoints her—most of her

The desert stars glittered overhead and a gentle breeze blew from the Sangre de Cristo Mountains as the couple said their wedding vows.

Mona Lisa Smile (2003)

students view their time at Wellesley as a steppingstone to a proper marriage. Betty Warren (Kirsten Dunst) is the biggest believer in a woman's "traditional" role, and becomes Katherine's most vocal adversary. Joan Brandwyn (Julia Stiles), Betty's best friend, is torn between marrying her boyfriend and applying to law school.

True to her (reported) promise to her husband, Danny was the film's second cameraman, under director Mike Newell (*Four Weddings and a Funeral*). To prepare for the role, Julia went to a '50s etiquette "boot camp" to learn how women were expected to behave in those times. She learned to dance the swing and the cha-cha, as well as the delicate of flirting—which sounds a little like King Kong taking ape lessons.

But every time it looks as if Julia has matured, she reverts to her old ways. During the shoot, she had a bizarre and somewhat hostile meeting with the local press. Geoff Edgers, who writes for the *Globe,* referred to Julia at the media conference as "snitty woman."

There were also reports of Julia flying into a rage when she thought that Danny and her co-star Kirsten Dunst were getting a little too friendly.

Columbia Pictures looked at Newell's final cut and went into raptures. They decided to delay the release of the film from July 11 to December 19, 2003, so as to be better positioned for Oscar consideration. But they need not have bothered. In *Mona Lisa Smile*, said one critic: "(The performers) are relegated to playing one-dimensional, uninteresting roles that could easily be dubbed the *Dead Poets Sorority.*" (This was in reference to the vastly superior Robin Williams film set in a boys' school.) But the film was critic-proof and just what audiences wanted to warm their Christmas dreams that year. *Mona Lisa Smile* was a big hit.

Julia was once again experiencing the euphoria that comes from surfing that big wave of public acceptance. And, at last, one of her great wishes was to be fulfilled. The small Moder family unit was about to double in size.

★☆★

chapter 14

Thirty Minutes of Wonderful

Julia and Danny Moder showed the public faces of marital bliss. But, when living life in the headlines, it is always difficult to separate fiction from truth. Married or not, Danny was a hunk and had a reputation for being something of a player even before Julia met him. Sometimes his past romantic life pushed into his current one. And, of course, Julia's track record was well known. The media speculated on Julia's need for children as well. After the first few months of their marriage, reports of her attending various fertility clinics emerged.

On May 31, 2004, Julia's unofficial magazine biographer, ***People***, scored the scoop—Julia was to give birth to twins, a boy and a girl.

On May 31, 2004, Julia's unofficial magazine biographer, *People*, scored the scoop—Julia was to give birth to twins, a boy and a girl. The tabloid press quickly jumped all over the story with reports of surprising veracity. Meanwhile, *Us* magazine scooped the world by revealing that a now-happy Vera Steinberg was eight months pregnant after "hooking up with an old flame."

There is something ironic in the fact that Cate Blanchett, who created the original role of the aloof photographer Anna, dropped out of Mike Nichols' film *Closer* because she was pregnant. *Closer*, a sexually frank, brutally funny play by Patrick Marber, opened in London's West End in 1998 and created quite a stir with its frequent use of four-letter words in a sexual roundelay between its four main characters.

Julia saw the play and was not impressed: "I didn't like it, not because it wasn't good, but because it was so ugly to me."

There is no nudity or simulated sex in *Closer* (either the play or the movie), but there is something much stronger—language—raw, obscene and shocking. The movie examines the shifting relationships between four characters: Larry (Clive Owen), a dermatologist with a hankering for kinky sex, Alice (Natalie Portman), a young woman whose waif-like appearance serves her well as a part-time stripper, Dan (Jude Law), a failed writer who is more in love with sex than love, and Anna (Julia), a photographer who really does not have any outstanding traits. Of all the characters, she is the most intelligent and normal and gets some of the best lines.

Julia may not have been director Mike Nichols' first choice, but she was an inspired second. She arrived on set knowing she was working with two of England's best actors and a fast-rising newbie. Portman, best known for her role as Senator Amidala in the *Star Wars* series, had burst onto the scene in 1994 as a precocious child taken under the wing of a professional hit man in the French film *The Professional.* Despite the high-profile, blue-ribbon cast and the possibility of a clash of egos, the players got down to the job and carried a low media profile.

Not one to say nice things for the sake of saying them, Nichols was particularly impressed with what Julia brought to the shoot.

Closer (2004)

JULIA FAN FACT

According to a study of Los Angeles plastic surgeons, there are two specific looks that patients request: Cindy Crawford and Julia Roberts.

"You can see what she is thinking," he said. "Her vulnerability and transparency is what makes her so accessible to audiences. It's Julia's immense professionalism that enabled her to take the role at short notice and that made us all confident she could and would do it," recalls Nichols. "For a star of her status, her work ethic is legendary."

Closer was released during the first week of December 2004. Some critics (and audiences) found it chilly, distant and uninvolving. But most loved it, setting off a widespread critical debate. A.O. Scott in the *New York Times* hailed Nichols as one of the few filmmakers "capable of infusing the bodily expressions of erotic desire with dramatic force and psychological meaning."

Julia Roberts had never been better in a dramatic film. For years, she had been the queen of romantic comedy, but with *Closer,* she tore into the material, and her maturity and world-weary sexuality placed her at the very center of the movie. Said Philip Wunch in the *Dallas Morning News*: "For the first time since *Pretty Woman*, you may actually forget that Julia Roberts is Julia Roberts."

Julia then went straight into the sequel to the high-tech comedy caper *Ocean's Eleven*, entitled *Ocean's Twelve*. The sequel was set three years after the original heist. Danny gathers his gang of con artists and thieves (and his wife) again, and they all jet off to Amsterdam, Rome and Paris to pull off three separate hits. (Part of the film was also shot in Clooney's $10 million mansion on the banks of Lake Como in Italy.) All the while,

Ocean's Twelve (2004)

the gang deals with increasing pressure from a very angry Terry Benedict (Andy Garcia as the casino boss they originally ripped off), as well as a dedicated Europol agent (Catherine Zeta-Jones) and a mysterious French rival known as the "Night Fox."

The group engaged in their usual high jinks, delighting the press wherever they stopped. They spent hours playing poker in basements and on rooftops—there were so many fans and media following them around, they couldn't leave their hotels. A British tourist, upon surveying the wild scene at Lake Como with television cameras, paparazzi, reporters, burly security guards and fans hanging around George Clooney's lakefront villa, could be excused for asking, "Is Bush here?"

George Clooney recalled that it was during the first month of shooting that Julia discovered she was pregnant. "We all knew we had to completely rethink her role," he told *Entertainment Weekly*. For early scenes, director Steven Soderbergh shot Roberts sitting down or blocked her body with furniture. Once her character got to Italy, however, Roberts had to be an essential part of a museum heist. Soderbergh came up with the idea of having Roberts' character, Tess, impersonate a pregnant Julia Roberts. Clooney says everyone loved the idea but wondered if "Julia was willing to do something as ballsy as that. We were asking her to make fun of herself or celebrity or whatever. It's a very hard thing to do because you're using yourself as the target, but Julia just jumped in with both feet."

> They spent hours playing poker in basements and on rooftops—there were so many fans and media following them around, they couldn't leave their hotels.

Julia told *Entertainment Weekly* that she had to augment her pregnancy with a pillow shoved up her dress. "It was more uncomfortable than my real pregnancy. Number one, it was square. And it was polyester. And it had, like, a little rhinestone thing on it that was always scratching." Even pregnant and dressing down, Julia made a much stronger impression than she had in the first film, and indeed, in the midst of some pretty tough company, she stole every scene she appeared in.

The film was released on December 10, 2004. The reviews were a bit more tepid than the ones that had welcomed the first film, but *Ocean's Twelve* immediately rose to the top of the box office lists.

Despite her physical exertions during the shooting of the film, Julia, on her doctor's orders, took things easy. Back home, she mostly puttered around her ranch. In early November, the star was rushed to the hospital with her husband Danny at her side, experiencing early contractions. They hooked her up to a fetal monitor and the contractions stopped. Her doctor ordered her to bed for the remainder of the pregnancy.

It was a bad time for Julia and her studios, though, with two movies yet to be released. But she would take no chances. Julia did a number of satellite and phone interviews from her ranch, telling her unseen interviewers: "I'm enormous." She added that the babies were "bionic. It's pretty amazing." She invited her old friend Oprah down with a crew for the only live interview she gave during her entire confinement. For a woman about to have two children, Julia looked radiant. She told Oprah she hadn't experienced any of the queasiness associated with morning sickness until she appeared on the show. It was caused, she thought, by the energy and applause from the audience. She went on to say

We were asking her to make fun of herself or celebrity or whatever. It's a very hard thing to do because you're using yourself as the target, but Julia just jumped in with both feet."

that her laugh was changing, making her sound like a hearty truck driver. Said Julia: "I find my pregnancy very empowering."

On Sunday morning, November 28, 2004, Julia Roberts gave birth, one month prematurely, to twins Hazel Patricia and Phinnaeus Walter Moder at an unnamed Southern California hospital. On that day, mother and babies were reported to be doing well.

With the release of two big movies and the birth of twins, it might be a good time to look and at the life of this conflicted, confounding and larger-than-life woman. Since her debut, Julia Roberts has established herself as one of the greatest stars in the history of Hollywood. She has lived her life in headlines, generating more copy than any other personality. When she gave birth to Hazel and Phinnaeus, the news was not hidden away in entertainment pages but was greeted with headlines and pictures in every major newspaper and telecast. Her movies are generally critic-proof—many of them coast to success just because her name is up there on the marquee. She is held in such high regard by her many fans that they will faithfully pay their money to see her in glossy but empty, big-budget studio behemoths, throw-away comedies and even small cameo roles.

Perhaps we love her because we feel we can see beyond the lights and camera, the wild nights of carousing and promiscuity, to the little girl growing up in a profoundly dysfunctional family in Smyrna, Georgia.

Of course, even her faithful fans didn't want to see her as the mousy Mary Reilly or as Michael Collins' girlfriend, but these were rough spots in a career that has always floated upwards. We seem to be able to forgive this woman anything in her personal life. Julia has set in motion a series of scandals that would have destroyed the career of a lesser luminary. Before her marriage to Danny Moder, she was a commitment phobic who turned away time and again from love. Perhaps we love her because we feel we can see beyond the lights and camera, the wild nights of carousing and promiscuity, to the little girl growing up in a profoundly dysfunctional family in Smyrna, Georgia.

Julia Roberts, even in the most sophisticated or down-and-dirty situation, projects a trembling vulnerability. When it comes right down to it, her appeal is not in overt sexiness or sophistication, but in the fact that she is lovable. You want to give her a hug and protect her from her own folly. She is her own most enduring creation—a dazzling movie superstar who is, at heart, just the girl next door.

★★★

JULIA ROBERTS FILMOGRAPHY

Ant Bully (2006)
Ocean's Twelve (2004)
Closer (2004)
Mona Lisa Smile (2003)
Confessions of a Dangerous Mind (2002)
Full Frontal (2002)
Grand Champion (2002)
Ocean's Eleven (2001)
America's Sweethearts (2001)
The Mexican (2001)
Erin Brokovich (2000)
Runaway Bride (1999)
Notting Hill (1999)
Stepmom (1998)
Conspiracy Theory (1997)
My Best Friend's Wedding (1997)
Everyone Says I Love You (1996)
Michael Collins (1996)
Mary Reilly (1996)
Something to Talk About (1995)

Prêt-à-Porter/Ready to Wear (1994)
I Love Trouble (1994)
The Pelican Brief (1993)
Hook (1991)
Dying Young (1991)
Sleeping with the Enemy (1991)
Flatliners (1990)
Pretty Woman (1990)
Steel Magnolias (1989)
Blood Red (1989)
Mystic Pizza (1988)
Baja Oklahoma (1988)
Satisfaction (1988)

Notes on Sources

Many of the quotes and some of the background information in this book come from interviews conducted by the author with Dylan McDermott, Shirley MacLaine, Sally Field, Richard Gere, Garry Marshall, Denzel Washington, Steven Spielberg, Nick Nolte, Catherine Zeta-Jones and Kiefer Sutherland. The above interviews were conducted about specific films and not necessarily in reference to this book.

Other sources include (but are not limited to):

Wallner, Rosemary. *Julia Roberts: Prettiest Woman.* Edina, Minnesota: Abdo & Daughters, 1991.

MacLaine, Shirley. *My Lucky Stars: A Hollywood Memoir.* New York: Bantam Books, 1996.

Donnelley, Paul. *Julia Roberts Confidential: The Unofficial Biography.* London: Virgin Books Ltd., 2003.

Spada, James. *Julia: Her Life.* New York: St. Martin's Press, 2004.

Taylor, Nancy. *Julia Roberts.* Harlow, England: Pearson Education Ltd., 2002.

★★★